THE GOSPEL according to THE WALL STREET JOURNAL

Carnegie Samuel Calian

JOHN KNOX PRESS
ATLANTA

Library of Congress Cataloging in Publication Data

Calian, Carnegie Samuel.
The gospel according to the Wall Street journal.

Includes bibliographical reference.
1. Wall Street journal. 2. Christianity and economics. 3. Christian life–1960- I. Title.
PN4899.N42W24 248'.9'5 74-19971
ISBN 0-8042-0826-3

Printed in the United States of America

to
DORIS

ACKNOWLEDGMENTS

Permission granted by *The Wall Street Journal* to include headlines and mini-quotes in this book.

Richard Easterlin, "Does Money Buy Happiness?" *The Public Interest,* Number 30 (Winter, 1973), pp. 3-10. Copyright© 1973 by National Affairs, Inc.

Permission granted by The Rockefeller Foundation to use quotations made by Paul Fruend at The Rockefeller Foundation Conference on "Values in Contemporary Society" (July 31, 1972).

Robert N. McMurray, "Power and the Ambitious Executive," Harvard Business Review, November–December 1973. Permission granted.

Malcolm Muggeridge. From the *Firing Line* transcript "Has America Had It?" September 16, 1973. Permission granted.

Articles previously published by Carnegie Samuel Calian and adapted for use in *The Gospel According to The Wall Street Journal:*

"Reviving the Church as an Institution." From *The Wall Street Journal*'s publication of April 20, 1973. Adapted and used in Chapter VI.

"The Theology of *The Wall Street Journal.*" Copyright© 1972 Christian Century Foundation. Reprinted by permission from the May 24, 1972 issue of *The Christian Century.* Adapted and used in Chapter II.

"How to Go Through Seminary Without Losing Your Faith." Copyright© 1973 Christian Century Foundation. Reprinted by permission from the February 7, 1973 issue of *The Christian Century.* Adapted and used in Chapter III.

"To Find Happiness." Copyright *Presbyterian Life.* Used by permission. Adapted and used in Chapter III.

"The Christian Who Came in from the Cold." Reprinted by permission from the May–June 1974 issue *The New Pulpit Digest.* Adapted and used in Chapter VI.

"Rich Nations and Poor Nations Need Each Other." Reprinted by permission from *New Catholic World,* January–February 1973. Adapted and used in Chapter V.

Contents

Preface 9

I. Discovering *The Wall Street Journal* 13

II. The *Journal*'s Gospel 25

III. The Nature of Radical Faith 33

IV. The Reader's World 47

V. The Neglected Side of the *Journal*'s Gospel 67

VI. Hope in a Watergate World 91

OTHER BOOKS BY C. S. CALIAN

The Significance of Eschatology in the Thoughts of Nicolas Berdyaev

Icon And Pulpit: The Protestant-Orthodox Encounter

Berdyaev's Philosophy of Hope

Grace, Guts and Goods: How to Stay Christian in an Affluent Society

CONTRIBUTING AUTHOR:

The New Man, Orthodox-Reformed Dialogue

Encyclopaedia Britannica

Preface

The Wall Street Journal is an important newspaper. This is a widely accepted fact in our society and abroad. The *Journal* is a symbol of our business culture, which permeates and influences the life-style of all institutions in American life.

We live in a business world; economics, budgets, and dollars often have the last word in determining our policies and programs throughout the structures of our society. A consumer-oriented public is becoming increasingly conscious of this pervasive economic umbrella covering us. The *Journal* highlights this fact. It contains within its pages the joys and frustrations resulting from this economic outlook on life. Its stories, articles, and news reports reflect the values, beliefs, goals, achievements, and shortcomings of our business culture.

The *Journal* receives credibility with its readership not only because of the quality of its product but also because it is a successful enterprise. Its very success embodies the aspirations and goals of a majority of our society. *The Gospel According to The Wall Street Journal* is the unfolding story of its success, based upon a no-nonsense philosophy of life. Common sense realism and firm commitment to individual hard work and creativity in the trials of life are the substance of its gospel.

The major thrust of the book is to examine the efficacy of the *Journal*'s gospel, questioning it, to see if it stands as an adequate philosophy of life within our complex, changing society. Hopefully, these pages will offer the reader a greater sense of purposefulness, as we strive individually and together to exercise the responsibilities demanded by the realities of our existence. Furthermore, this study is interested in helping readers to be more successful persons beyond material measurements, important as they are. It also wishes to show how personal success is dependent upon and related to our neighbor's quality of life in the global village.

Today, we are a super-rich nation, in danger of losing our souls and our genius for greatness due to our excessive comfort and lack of purpose. To morally and materially arrest this decay is a basic aim of this book. Another goal is to help us assume, through heightened consciousness, our new roles and responsibilities in this *one world* of ours. To this end, these pages hope to serve as a catalyst, causing us to have second thoughts on the good life, as we continue our pilgrimage for a truly more prosperous and meaningful tomorrow for ourselves and our loved ones.

To achieve these objectives, this study moves toward the following: (1) a focus upon the *Journal* as a key to our better understanding of the business culture and its influence upon us; (2) appraisal of this influence on our lives from the vantage point of a theologian and in the light of larger realities in our global society; and (3) some suggestive pointers toward furthering the quality of life for ourselves and for those around us.

The book's concluding note asks that we look beyond the *Journal*'s gospel to a more encompassing message of hope in a Watergate world, found in a radical faith symbolized in the cross of Christ.

The completion of this book would not have been possible without the cooperation and encouragement of many persons and organizations. To cite only a few and run the risk of slighting others, I wish to extend a special thanks for the courtesies extended to mc by the staff of *The Wall Street Journal.* My candid conversations with some of the staff have given to the *Journal* a "human face."

For a better understanding of our business community, I am appreciative of opportunities for spending several weeks with Interstate Power Company and the Dubuque Packing Company. The insights and activities of corporate life and business practices were quite instructive. My interviews and lengthy conversations with businessmen and professionals in the community were a continual source of insight and information, for which I am grateful. In addition, my speaking engagements with various professional associations and business groups and the resulting exchanges which took place added to my perceptions, as did the seminar I conducted on "Christianity in a Business World" attended by leaders from the business community. Thanks also go to my students, a constant source of challenge, and to my colleagues at the University of

Dubuque for their lessons that the college and the seminary are also parts of the business world.

My contacts through the Academy for Contemporary Problems in Columbus, Ohio, and the invitation to participate at the "Markets and Morals Conference" sponsored by Battelle at its Seattle Research Center provided many lively moments of intellectual excitement and a widening of my own horizons.

In concluding this preface, I would like to express my indebtedness to Peg Saunders for the typing of the manuscript, to my wife, Doris, for her critical and helpful reading of the manuscript, and to the editor, Richard Ray of John Knox Press, who initiated this project and whose patience, understanding, and suggestions have been most supportive toward the completion of this undertaking.

C. S. Calian
Dubuque, Iowa

1

Discovering *The Wall Street Journal*

It would almost seem presumptuous to suggest that *The Wall Street Journal* needs to be discovered. [illegible] is widely acclaimed in the United States and beyond [illegible] respected, most influential [illegible] today. [illegible] *Journal* [illegible] that there is no doubt [illegible] of the Western [illegible].

You may ask, why would a [illegible] who discusses [illegible] minister preaching in a [illegible] and *The Wall Street Journal*? Does [illegible] a financial sheet for [illegible]? According to the *Journal*'s own account, 87% of all [illegible] earning $25,000 or more read the newspaper every business day. Furthermore, among America's top 750 companies, [illegible]. The *Journal* is also [illegible] $30,000 or more.

It should be pointed out in passing that *The Wall Street Journal* is actually a part of a larger enterprise, the Dow Jones & Co., which publishes [illegible] *Barron's Weekly* and [illegible] Dow Jones News Service [illegible] which in turn publishes [illegible] Sunday newspapers. How [illegible] *The Wall Street Journal* [illegible] effective decentralization [illegible] printing centers based upon a [illegible] printing system, which enables [illegible] printed in 12

I

Discovering *The Wall Street Journal*

It would almost seem ludicrous to suggest that *The Wall Street Journal* needs to be discovered. The *Journal* is widely acclaimed in the United States and beyond as the *most trusted, most profitable,* and *most powerful* newspaper in existence today. Yet, the *Journal* was unknown to me until a short time ago. That was due, no doubt, to personal circumstances and was not the fault of the *Journal.*

You may ask, why would a theologian who discusses God and "spiritual affairs," an ordained Presbyterian minister teaching in a theological seminary, wish to read *The Wall Street Journal*? Doesn't the *Journal* convey the image of being essentially a financial sheet for businessmen? According to the *Journal*'s own account, 51% of all businessmen earning $25,000 or more read the newspaper every business day. Furthermore, among America's top 750 companies, the *Journal* is read by 83% of all company officers and by 77% of all executives in the manufacturing companies. The *Journal* is also read by 88% of all executives earning $50,000 or more.

It should be mentioned in passing that *The Wall Street Journal* is actually a part of a larger enterprise known as the Dow Jones & Co., which publishes, in addition to the *Journal, Barron's Weekly,* and *The National Observer.* It also operates the Dow Jones News Service and owns the Ottaway Newspaper Group, which in turn publishes twelve general-circulation dailies and five Sunday newspapers. Dow Jones derives 65% of its revenue from *The Wall Street Journal.* A major reason for the *Journal*'s success is the effective decentralized printing centers. There are now ten printing centers based upon a microwave facsimile transmission and offset printing system, which enables the *Journal* to be the major national newspaper in the country. Internationally, the *Journal*'s accomplishment is outdistanced only by the publication of *Pravda. Pravda* is printed in 42 different locations across the Soviet Union; photographs of pages are sent by cable and satellite to those areas farthest from Moscow.

Due to its technically advanced capacity for distribution and reliability, the *Journal*'s readership continues to grow each year. Today's readers number nearly four and one-half million persons, which Dow Jones & Company boasts to its advertisers as being an A+ quality readership. An advertisement appearing on January 25, 1974 under the title "The Penalty of Readership" reads . . .

> So today, when advertisers recognize the value of effective readership, we don't have to slice, cut, or chop our audience into "A", "B", "C" groups.
>
> An advertiser can buy any one, or any combination, of our four regional editions, but we've made sure that no matter which he buys, he gets the best.
>
> Because we offer only one kind of readership: A+.
>
> And we've never penalized our advertisers by delivering any other kind.

The quality of such high readership commands hefty charges for advertising, and the *Journal* profitably obliges. In 1972, a full-page ad in the *Journal* cost $20,957, more than double the amount charged by *The New York Times.* The *Journal* justifies the high rates by the affluence of its audience, since, as the above ad claims, the readership is A+. The average annual income among this readership is $33,761 (taken from 1971 *Annual Report* of Dow Jones & Company), and one-half of the total number of readers are employed in professional or managerial occupations, including 173,380 presidents of companies. What, you might well ask, is a theologian doing among this select group of the economic elite? What would a theologian have in common with the editors or with an A+ readership of a newspaper designed to reach those far beyond his income level? The answer to these and other questions I wish to raise is what this book is all about.

Symbol of Success

The Wall Street Journal is not only a symbol of the Establishment, it is even more a symbol of success. My own discovery of this fact began when certain acquaintances of mine—businessmen and professionals—had made it clear to me that this was an important newspaper to read if the motivation and aspirations of countless Americans were to be understood. In fact, said one friend, "I read *The Wall Street Journal* and my Bible together daily." My thoughts pondered—*The Wall Street Journal* and the Bible—was there some relationship between the two? The *Journal* might well be the "Bible of Business," but was it also serving as an interpreter of Scripture for some? Or was it the other way around—was the Bible serving as an interpretative guide over the news and opinions contained in the *Journal*? These questions began to intrigue me, and my acquaintances nurtured my curiosity with their day old copies of the *Journal.* This went on for some time, until I found myself genuinely looking forward to reading the interesting, well-written and researched feature stories, editorial opinions, articles, and news capsules contained in the *Journal.* I was also amazed to observe that in this age of multi-media, the *Journal* is published without pictures—its illustrations are essentially its feature stories. It wasn't long before I took out my own subscription and joined the rank of A+ readership. Thus began my dialogue with the *Journal.*

What did I discover? Among the varied and surprising themes found in the *Journal*, I unexpectedly found familiar theological terms such as God, guilt, sin, redemption, creation, etc. freely employed in the stories, articles, and especially in the editorial opinions found in the *Journal.* I started a file, clipping articles whenever such terms or themes conveying a theological sense were used. My file grew rapidly. Then, on January 17, 1972, in memory of their late editor, William H. Grimes (1941-58), the *Journal* republished his statement written in 1951 entitled, "A Newspaper's Philosophy." Grimes wrote:

> On our editorial page we make no pretense of walking down the middle of the road. Our comments and interpretations are made from a definite point of view. We believe in the individual, in his wisdom and his decency. We oppose all infringements on individual rights, whether they stem from attempts at private monopoly, labor union monopoly or from an overgrowing government. People will say we are conservative or even reactionary. We are not much interested in labels but if we were to choose one, we would say we are radical. Just as radical as the Christian doctrine.

Taking Grimes' quote as my clue, I proceeded then to reread all the materials collected in my file. From that study, a theological profile began to emerge, which was first published in an article in *The Christian Century* entitled "The Theology of *The Wall Street Journal*," and subsequently published in a more abbreviated version in *Intellectual Digest* and the *Journal* itself. I was then invited by John Knox Press to expand the theme into its present book form. As part of my research on the book, I had opportunities to visit the New York offices of the *Journal*, where I was graciously received.

During the course of my conversation with staff members, I found both a spirit of confidence and competence toward their work. While there were no "liberals" on the editorial staff, there was the genuine concern to study issues from more than one perspective. The editorial page editor, Robert L. Bartley, continues the Iowa dynasty on that page and reflects the mid-America mores and concern for balance and perspective. There is a great deal of freedom for the reporters in producing investigative stories that express the facts and the issues involved. The *Journal*'s staff is well aware that a large measure of their success among their readership is based upon the factor of trustworthy information. An image of trust has been vital to success. Unlike most business publishers who are tempted to inflate corporate successes, the *Journal* provides its readers with unadulterated information on which they can rely. The caliber and dedication of the staff toward truthful journalism is the force behind the quality of reliability that has been expected and found in the *Journal*.

The *Journal*'s biggest problem is that it is too successful and risks becoming complacent; such have been the sentiments expressed by the *Journal*'s vice president, Edward R. Cony. No doubt this is a danger for any organization. There was a time, however, when the *Journal* was not so successful; in the Depression its circulation fell to under 30,000. Thanks to the Dow Jones ticker, which managed to stay profitable, the *Journal* avoided failure.

The *Journal*'s climb to fame and fortune is well in keeping with the American idea of success. Charles H. Dow, Edward D. Jones, and Charles M. Bergstressor, the founders, were responsible for converting their newsletter into a newspaper, which typified the American drive for success. The publication on July 8, 1889, of Vol.

1, No. 1 of *The Wall Street Journal* was the culmination of New England ingenuity, thrift, hard work, and the foresight for acquisition. By 1902, Clarence W. Barron (for whom the *Journal*'s sister publication is named) bought the company from its founders. Following Barron's death in 1928, Jane, his stepdaughter, and her husband, Hugh Bancroft, took control of the paper.* In 1933 Kenneth C. Hogate succeeded Bancroft as president. Hogate made the decision to broaden the paper's appeal, and under the leadership of Bernard (Barney) Kilgore, the real boost to the paper's future began in 1941. Included in this new team that gave *The Wall Street Journal* its present image were William H. Grimes, William F. Kerby, Buren McCormack, and Robert Bottorff. Kerby is currently the chairman of the board and Warren H. Phillips the president. Phillips' selection is a break in the long standing tradition of Protestant, Midwest stock which has prevailed in the higher echelons of the *Journal.* Phillips is the son of a Jewish slip manufacturer from Queens and considers himself a Unitarian. Phillips, like his predecessors, is also committed to the American idea of success.

As one of the most trusted, most profitable, and most powerful newspapers in the world today, *The Wall Street Journal* is an obvious symbol of success. Designed to reach aspiring and successful individuals, the *Journal* is the very symbol of the goal its readership wishes to attain. Is this image conveyed by the *Journal* desirable? Is the message of this book simply to buy and study this newspaper in order to become successful? Are the *Journal*'s observations on society, life, and its overall philosophy a model to follow in our organizations and personal lives? In short, is the *Journal*'s "gospel" good news or bad news?

---

*Today, the controlling stockholders at Dow Jones are Mrs. William C. Cox and Mrs. A. Werk Cook, daughters of Jane Barron Bancroft. They own 36 percent of the stock, while other members of the Bancroft family own another 28 percent of the stock.

See *Well Beyond the Average, The Story of Dow Jones & Company, Inc.* published by Dow Jones. Also of interest are the following articles: "One Story *The Wall Street Journal* Won't Print," by Carol J. Loomis, *Fortune,* August, 1971 and "Up Against *The Wall Street Journal*" by A. Kent Macdougall, *MORE, A Journalism Review,* October, 1972.

A Historical Footnote

Before we can answer any of the above questions, it's necessary that we develop an extended historical footnote to appreciate the larger framework in which the *Journal* operates. I am not referring now to the journalistic world to which it belongs, but rather to an understanding of success which we and the *Journal* have inherited. The *Journal*'s symbol of success is actually tied to the historical and theological values of our heritage.

It's true that we are a *here and now* people. It's never easy to see ourselves in historical perspective. At times, it takes visitors from abroad to help us gain a focus on ourselves. Gunnar Myrdal, the well-known Swedish scholar, has observed that collectively as a people, we Americans worship success. Is that a fair appraisal of ourselves? No doubt the idea of success does run in the very bloodstream of our nation, for we regard our nation itself as a success. Our bicentennial celebration is an expression of that success. Many of the clergy in our nation's history have encouraged us to believe in a God who wishes us to be successful, so that the very success image of Americans is rooted in religious motivation.

Charles Dow, Edward Jones, and Clarence Barron were well saturated with this religious motivation for success from their New England heritage. This heritage dates from the Reformation, which taught that the chief end of man was to glorify God and do his will. Doing the "will of God" within our Puritan framework meant hard work, thrift, saving, and the slow acquisition of wealth. The will of God in practice meant the *economic* will of God. Almost literally, the quest for the will of God became a quest for wealth. Did the acquiring of wealth spell success for Americans? The story of Dow Jones & Company, Inc., in the very title of their booklet, *Well Beyond the Average,* attempts to answer the question for many. Yet, are we satisfied with this answer? The constant dialogue between the front page features in the *Journal* and the opinions and articles on the editorial page reveals the search for a more satisfying answer.

This pursuit for a more satisfying answer historically can be traced from Ben Franklin's *Poor Richard's* maxims to the Horatio Alger stories, from Russell Conwell's *Acres of Diamonds* to Bruce

Barton's *The Man Nobody Knows* to Norman Vincent Peale's *Power of Positive Thinking*. Success for Americans has generally meant making money and translating it into status or fame. Success was essentially measurable in terms of money or applause (e.g., an Andrew Carnegie or a Mark Twain). Success was the process of *attaining* riches or *achieving* fame—you had to know the person's starting point and where he ended to determine whether the individual was successful. The roots of the American spirit were based upon the building of a fortune or the building of a reputation. The lead stories in the *Journal* on personalities and companies oscillate between these two major themes—the rise or fall of someone's fortune or fame.

This whole drama is vividly seen in our own social lives. Success requires us to change our friends at times, as does failure. For example, "What better way was there of measuring the pace of keeping up with the Joneses than by getting ahead of the Browns by getting in with the Smiths?" This is from historian Richard M. Huber, whose study, *The American Idea of Success* (p. 8, McGraw-Hill, 1971), indicates that "getting ahead" has been a sacred American slogan. This is why Americans often appear so "pushy" to persons abroad. It is also why many other nationalities appear "lazy" or "sluggish" through our filter.

America has been historically a nation of *social climbers*. Those who have "arrived" in American life are looked upon as economic elite, judged by the quality of their homes, the number and type of cars, memberships to exclusive clubs, etc. "Bettering oneself" is our working creed, not necessarily the Apostles' Creed that is repeated each Sunday in our churches. "You can't keep a good man down" is the standard cliché when one is faced with setbacks in the process of "bettering oneself." The human interest film *Sounder* contained this note as one of its themes. The film is the story of a Southern black sharecropper family seeking to survive during the Depression, while the eldest child, David Lee, struggles to improve his lot through education.

What really scares today's economic elite is the apparent "greening of America." The rejection of our aspirations and values by our own children threatens us especially at those private moments when we indulge in introspective self-doubt. For the most part, we try hard to stamp out from our minds our doubts and anxieties. However, the one-page ad in the *Journal* recommending "What to do if your kid is a hippie" did not go unnoticed. The sponsor of the ad was sensitive to the concerns of the readership of the paper. On the other side of the ledger, the apparent "greening" has led to the "blueing" of America. That is to say, opportunity for the advancement of blue collar children like the David Lees has increased today, due in part to the drop-out rate of affluent children who refuse to buy into their parents' way of life.

The drive for success operates on two tracks in our society, with some degree of overlapping. The two tracks are these: success which is profit-oriented and success which is nonprofit-oriented. Businessmen and professionals—engineers, doctors, lawyers, architects, managers, bankers, etc.—are interested in rendering a service with a profit. Ministers, teachers, social workers, professors, etc., also render a service for non-profit. There are, of course, some ministers, like Norman Vincent Peale, who have made a fortune in a nonprofit profession. There are also medical missionaries like an Albert Schweitzer or Tom Dooley who have labored for no profit. In fact, what often captures the imagination of a local church is to support a medical missionary, since the congregation can readily grasp the financial sacrifice the doctor is making. Whichever track is pursued, the drive for success exists. There is a "profit and loss column" for the clergyman within his parameters as there is for the businessman within his parameters.

Standards of Success

In practice, what have been the standards of success in American life? Recognition of success is far more complicated than many of us admit. Success for one party may be failure for another and vice versa. The church, for the most part, has always protected itself regarding success. The church calls those who have been successful Christians "saints." This happens after the individual is dead. Society, on the other hand, seeks to recognize success during life—awarding Oscars, bonuses, Nobel prizes, recognition in *Who's Who in America,* etc. It may well be that successful persons once honored may in retrospect be viewed as questionable characters.

What then are the standards of success? According to the Horatio Alger stories, the ideal career in America began by being born a poor boy who struggled essentially unaided against overwhelming odds until attaining the top of his occupation. After all, isn't America the "land of opportunity"? That cliché, of course, may be questioned, depending upon one's status, sex, or race. But for the majority of males with white skin, this is certainly the "land of opportunity." I well remember my immigrant parents' exhortation, "Remember to thank God each day that you were born in America." The typical success story in American life, as in Dow Jones & Company, followed this usual scenario—struggle to get ahead, acquire, expand, and then give away—as in the grand style of Andrew Carnegie, John Rockefeller, Commodore Vanderbilt, Daniel Drew, and many others.

The secret of success was summed up in Russell Conwell's *Acres of Diamonds*—a sermon-lecture which he delivered some 6,000 times. The essence of the story is that you don't have to look everywhere, only in your own backyard, to discover worthwhile opportunities pointing to a successful and wealthy life. There are "acres of diamonds" in your very home town, if you have the vision and will to reach for them. Whether your drive for success was for profit or non-profit, the aspirations of either agreed on the need for struggle; the worse curse was to be born the son of a rich man. If you were poor, you would be forced to overcome obstacles and forge ahead. One can see then how the frontier mentality and the drive for success converged as powerful allies in the ambitious person's climb to success.

When it almost seemed that success American-style was a well-established pattern, the sophisticated citizen discovered that reaching material success did not satisfy his deeper longings nor quiet the restlessness within himself. In the second half of the 19th and into the 20th century, writers and popularizers began to speak of seeking not mere material success, but "true success." *True success* pointed beyond possessions, status, and fame. True success was seen in terms of character development, happiness, and improved human relationships. Dale Carnegie's *How to Win Friends and Influence*

People became a bible for many. Finding true success or happiness was doing good to others without pragmatic considerations, finding peace of mind, experiencing the joy of living, basking in the love of friends and family, trying your best without having to win, doing your thing, serving God, getting along with people, and simplifying your life–style.

There arose the sudden realization that the above–mentioned characteristics might well be in direct conflict with the requirements of becoming materially successful. If real life calls for competition, aggressiveness, impersonal and selfish existence, while true success calls for gentleness, forgiveness, sacrifice, and brotherly love, are we then faced with a conflict?

Many Americans made the self-discovery that successful economics does not promise happiness, especially if the race to material success has included infighting that has dehumanized us in the process. Authentic human relationships and friendships often become a luxury that the successful individual cannot afford.

For example, a group of executives attending a training session was asked to write down their ambitions and goals for the future. The conference leader then suggested that each participant choose another member of the group to regard as a friend and share these ambitions with him. "Hell," said one executive, "I don't have any friends; that's why I'm successful." The successful person often had to settle for counterfeit relationships rather than the real thing as the price for success.

What does such an attitude do for human relationships? Are we breaking apart as a society in our quest for success? Historian Huber noted, "we don't meet heart to heart anymore, we meet at cocktail parties in a superficial way. We value smartness rather than depth, shine rather than spirit. But I think people are sick of it, they want to get out of it." Changing a life-style is never easy, and often when it does take place it is too late to make any difference.

The advocates of true success nevertheless declare that it's never too late to learn that the best things in life can't be bought nor fully earned, such as a healthy body, inherited abilities and talents, a spouse's love and loyalty, the embrace of a child, and work that is regarded as play.

Success American-style presents us today with the unsavory paradox of achieving tangible goals while remaining restless, acquiring material success without happiness, experiencing the good things of life but not the good life. *The good things of life do not necessarily add up to the good life; success does not necessarily equal happiness.* Once realizing this, each American finds himself looking for the best possible compromise—making appropriate trade-offs and bargains for whatever pay-offs deemed desirable. Thus, as Huber's study has indicated, "the American idea of success at times has been a self-defeating mechanism for true happiness, an engine of discontent incessantly pushing expectations ahead of satisfaction." Knowing the dilemma we face, we continue to pay the price, striving to be winners today, but possibly losers in the end.

When pressed, the individual American would say that success should be defined in nonmaterialistic terms. However, collectively, as a society, Americans go on measuring success by a materialistic criterion of rewards. Herein lies our crisis and our tragedy as a great nation celebrating our bicentennial anniversary. Imbedded in the American way of life is this basic *dualism*—the materialism of success vs. the idealism of true success. This essential dualism explains how American culture can be both materialistic and at the same time deeply spiritual. Caught within this tension, we will go on with the game of life—doing what it takes to become a winner in society and possibly in the course of our race denying ourselves the gift of being truly human beings—enjoying the good life in community with each other.

The Wall Street Journal in its own style exemplifies the American idea of success. The *Journal* expresses well in its stories and opinions this basic dualism in our culture. Herein lies its interest for me as a theologian. To what extent is this dualism healthy and necessary, and to what extent is it sickly and dangerous? To what degree is it wise for us to attempt to reduce the tension between the material criteria for success and the idealistic criteria for success? Finally, how great is our determination to continue beyond our bicentennial to become more truly "one nation under God, with liberty and justice for all"? The next chapter will provide the *Journal*'s guidelines to these questions.

II

The *Journal*'s Gospel

Let's examine William H. Grimes' statement that those associated with *The Wall Street Journal* "are not much interested in labels, but if we were to choose one, we would say we are radical—just as radical as the Christian doctrine." This claim needs further study.

Presumably, Grimes' words, which appeared first in 1951 on the front page of the *Journal* and were republished in 1972 at the time of his death, express the outlook of the present editorial staff as well. A newspaperman's philosophy, like any other person's, has theological implications. The presuppositions behind the normal process of living should be filtered out and reviewed from time to time. We are reflective creatures, not robots, though at times our routines are mechanical. As a consequence, we often neglect our need for reflection. Victimized by our own *busyness,* we wonder what life is all about. Wisdom beckons us to examine the substructures on which our actions are based. Often our conscious awareness of these substructures, or presuppositions of our daily existence scares us and even reveals our cynicism and lack of faith in human nature. The *Journal* as a responsible paper attempts to replay our attitudes and behavior through its feature stories and editorial opinions. The editorials in particular seek to consciously bring to the forefront the assumptions behind our actions and to cast them into responsible perspective. The perspective the *Journal* casts is its philosophy, or what I prefer to call its theology.

In the normal course of living, the terms *philosophy* and *theology* are interwoven: one person's philosophy may be another individual's theology, and vice versa. That is to say, in the experience of living, human wisdom and divine revelation mysteriously converge and blend. Behind theological assumptions are philosophic presup-positions, and behind philosophic assumptions are theological presuppositions. One's philosophy of life (or theology of life more accurately) points to one's area(s) of ultimate concern—his de facto "god," if you will. To speak of a theology of life (rather than philosophy of life) is to refer then to the areas of ultimate concern for you. Thus it was no accident that editor Grimes compared his newspaper's philosophy to Christian doctrine. The *Journal*'s philosophy does indeed contain a theology, one that surfaces in editor Grimes' words "as radical as the Christian doctrine." That phrase is a declaration of faith.

Realities: God, Man & Society

What are the main features of *The Wall Street Journal*'s faith, its gospel? First, that God is not dead—at least not on its editorial page. It perceives the face of God as symbolized by man's drive for transcendence and for order, and by his capacity to work rationally and in a spirit of good will for the coming of the kingdom of God on earth. For example, in an editorial titled "Antidote for Anomie?" (April 23, 1968), the *Journal* sees religion as the answer to modern man's "restlessness-in-affluence." Certainly, it says, this restlessness testifies to a human craving for something transcendent. People today may not be much concerned about personal immortality, but they do want meaning and order in their lives. They are in quest of meaning and of the confidence and sense of self-worth that come with it. According to the *Journal*, the task of church and synagogue is to satisfy this God-hunger so prevalent in the marketplace. But unhappily, the *Journal* says, today's clergymen have apparently abandoned their primary task.

In any case, the *Journal* holds, each man's discovery that God is alive carries the promise of inner fulfillment. Says the editorial mentioned above: "Nothing the behavioralist psychologists have discovered in their rat mazes, for instance, will tell you as much about human nature as will the Judaeo-Christian view of man, created in the image of God but marred by original sin." A surprising theological observation, coming as it does not from a volume of systematic theology but from the editorial page of one of the country's leading financial newspapers. Indeed, for many persons the *Journal* serves as both a politico-economic and a Biblical commentary on contemporary affairs. The *Journal* is not sure that "the truths of religious tradition can be interpreted to satisfy this need" for "an antidote for anomie." But it is sure "that here, not in political activism, is religion's path to new relevance."

A second feature of the *Journal*'s gospel follows from the first: since God is not dead, neither is man eternally damned. Man is certainly imperfect, but he is not without hope. He can find his way through the dark tunnels of life, for there is always a shaft of light to guide him. Whatever we call it—reason, intuition or the capacity for good—there is a gleam that beckons us on, though we often stumble as we pursue it. Thus the *Journal* declares, in an editorial titled "Reflections on the Madness of the Age" (September 14, 1970), that "the human race has not suddenly plunged into the abyss; the horrors of irrationality have always ridden side by side with the wonders of spiritual and artistic accomplishment." The *Journal* goes on to say that "the traditional optimism must yet appear unfounded. It is just that now our age is learning, as all thinking people who have gone before us have had to learn, that fulfilling the promise takes a great deal more doing than once we had dreamed." In this as in many other editorials the *Journal* takes an essentially optimistic view of man's ability to cope with the almost insurmountable national and global problems he confronts.

Moreover, the *Journal* declares, man is responsible for his actions, and when he is found guilty he must make restitution. Thus, in "Second Thoughts on Lt. Calley" (April 7, 1971), the *Journal* says:

> The President would serve us well if he articulated the things that ought to become those sober second thoughts: that a civilized people will proceed not in anger, but in sorrow, but that there are some acts the nation cannot allow to go unpunished.

In another editorial, "Accountability and Arrogance," (May 3, 1971) the *Journal* raises the same point in regard to John Mitchell, the former attorney general, and Richard Helms, director of the CIA. These men's insistence that, "in the interest of national security," promiscuous wire-tapping was necessary the *Journal* calls "inexcusable." Since in a democracy no one person or group, however upstanding, always has the necessary wisdom to wield power responsibly, accountability for power is of the utmost importance. What emerges here is a theology of responsibility. Man, created in the image of God, has the capacity to do good; but since he is also victimized by circumstances beyond his control—the war in Vietnam, the loss of privacy through technology, etc.—his best efforts can be undermined. Nevertheless, awareness of his limitations does not render him the less responsible, in whatever situation. And though the *Journal* frankly admits ("Environment: the Human Element," September 1, 1970) that in the final analysis the human dimension is at the center of every problem, it still holds that man is accountable for what happens to society and the world.

Third, as a consequence of its affirmation of God and man, the *Journal's* gospel acknowledges *a rational order of social existence.* Fortunately, there are in every society morally sensitive people of good will who struggle day by day to create order out of chaos, to bring about a global society favoring peace rather than war. But the *Journal* constantly warns that, since even the best of men are imperfect, they may promote an illusory, unrealistic peace. In other words, it speaks for a realistic gospel about human society while it hopes for a community of good will.

More specifically, the *Journal* acknowledges that neither reason nor intuition—those sparks of the divine in man—can avail in all situations. Life is full of surprises and unexplained tragedies. That is why we must avoid "the search for simplistic solutions" (the title of an editorial in the April 30, 1971 issue). For instance, in answer to complaints about the slowness of integration, the *Journal* says:

> . . . it is no useful answer to try to engineer an instant end to discrimination, especially with public housing. The history of such projects in too many cities has shown that they often become instant new slums . . .
>
> Government can and should strike down legal segregation where it exists, but an end to discrimination depends on a slow buildup of good will, not a lot of artificial social engineering.

Obviously, however, the *Journal's* insistence on "realism" depends on what it considers "realistic." This is a matter of interpretation. One "realistic" appraiser of the state of society may recommend "artificial social engineering" or even revolutionary action; another appraiser, equally "realistic," may counsel a conservative, reactionary response to the same situation. The fact is that the filter through which we view life actually reveals our theological stance. For the *Journal*, this is the best of all possible worlds, and we are commissioned to maintain it and to work consciously and cautiously to eradicate the injustices and inequalities in human society. But since the *Journal* is practical in its outlook, it warns that justice and equality may be beyond our reach and insists that to think otherwise is to be naïve.

The *Journal* naturally wishes everyone to be a winner. This wish, of course, is a projection of its idealized view of the free (i.e., competitive) economic system, in which there is no substitute for winning. Realistically, however, the *Journal* knows that society consists of winners and losers. Thus it seems at times to display a placid acceptance of our divisions and problems. In the editorial "Shattered Illusions" (February 11, 1971) there is an indication that there will always be the rich and the poor, the healthy and the sick. Government subsidies, it points out, "only create the illusion of health, not health itself. And by the time the illusion is exposed, as it inevitably must be, the true condition is more likely to have deteriorated than to have improved." It is these costly illusions that the *Journal*'s editors fear above all; surrender to illusions is modern man's abyss.

Avoid illusions, be realistic—this is the golden rule implicit in many *Journal* editorials. Thus the paper claims ("The Impact of Change," May 3, 1971) that "reasonable severance pay, relocation and retraining will still be more appealing to many workers than the preservation of useless jobs." As to management, it exhorts executives to be deaf to the "call of the wild" (title of an editorial, March 1, 1971). The *Journal* acknowledges that today's problems and pressures are so great that many business executives—and indeed most people—are tempted at some time or other to abandon all responsibilities and heed the "call of the wild." Some yield to the temptation and seek a simpler life. "But surely something should be said for the resoluteness of those who, seeing those same shortcomings of society, endeavor to alleviate them within a context of freedom, order and civility."

Vested Interests

However, the *Journal* always sees illusion and realism in terms of vested interest, that being the filter through which they are identified. For example, in a favorable response to the Nixon administration's reversal of our China policy ("Is the World Coming to Its Senses?" July 19, 1971), the paper declares that "the world is war weary, sick of actual war and the threat of war," and suggests that this weariness has come because of instant communication—we now have "war in living (dying) color, and because of the new sense of global closeness induced by the explorations of space." To be sure, this editorial recognizes that the violent and gory history behind us hardly supports the hope of prolonged concern for peace in the future. "But for quite practical reasons, mankind's chance of avoiding extinguishing itself does look a little better this morning."

While accepting the change in our China policy, however, the *Journal* reacts negatively to other changes. In "A Christmas Present for the Young" (December 24, 1970), it objects to the enfranchisement of 18-year-olds. The right to vote, it says, is cherished by those who hold it, and comments: "We trust that the young will be wiser in their use of this Christmas present than their elders were in the giving of it." Again, in "The Basics of Integration" (January 26, 1972), the *Journal* opposes such innovations as ethnic quotas and school busing on the ground that these run counter to the American tradition. "That tradition, so successful in integrating ethnic groups into the larger society, has been that such groups are recognized in informal ways but not formal ones, that society will be pluralistic and the law will be color blind." All these editorials show how thin the line is between dreams and realities. But the *Journal*'s judgment of which is which is arrived at through the vested-interests filter in the eyes of the beholder.

Common Sense vs. the Cross

In the light of these editorials, the *Journal*'s theological stance can be defined. It calls for faith in a God who wills order, in man as an essentially moral and hopeful being, and in a society of persons—of persons who, limited by their sins, nevertheless have the power to ennoble themselves, to reveal the image of God hidden within each of them. The phrase, "moral man and immoral society," used by Reinhold Niebuhr as a book title (Charles Scribner's Sons, 1932) aptly describes the *Journal*'s outlook on life. The book suggests that the individual has the capacity to act morally apart from the larger social and economic problems.

The *Journal* is well aware that money and the material goods it buys do not satisfy all human needs. Money doesn't buy love or friendship or any warm human relationship; neither does it capture the experience of beauty or worship, or promote the pursuit of the true and the good. Recognizing all that, the *Journal* nevertheless insists on material needs. Money is a necessity for creating, for building, for exchanging goods and services—which is to say that the paper's editors are confessing materialists who affirm both the creation and the Creator of our Judeo-Christian tradition. But, as editor Grimes said, the *Journal* cannot be easily labeled. Like most local churches or synagogues, its editorials present a wide spectrum of opinion. It is doubtful, however, that Grimes was right in his description of *The Wall Street Journal* as "just as radical as the Christian doctrine." Did he realize the implications of that comparison? What is radical about Christian doctrine?

Radical Christian doctrine is best represented at *the cross*. And neither *The Wall Street Journal* nor the institutional church can call itself "radical" in the sense of the cross. The *Journal* is committed to a cautious, common-sense outlook on life. Such a commitment is essentially conservative in that whether those who make it call themselves conservatives or liberals, it usually leads to defense of the status quo with slight modifications.

From the vantage point of the cross, the *Journal* is no more interested than the institutional church (which the *Journal* considers too socially active) in being "radical." To be radical is to take the risk of being crucified, and that is hardly common sense. We practice a Christianity without a cross. Obsessed with the desire for happy endings, we run frantically from suffering. We try to simplify our lives, or (via tranquilizers) to jump off the dizzying merry-go-round pursuit of material comforts. Obedient to an unconscious drive to keep the harsher realities in bounds, we absorb more fiction than is healthy for us; for there seems to be a limit to the amount of nonfiction we can tolerate. Thus we abandon the gospel of the cross for a gospel of "realism," whose norm is common sense.

This gospel is grounded in self-interest, in the desire to survive at all costs. Both the *Journal* and the institutional church understand the requirements of self-interest. So those of us who are church people forget that Christian theology is a pilgrim theology. Long ago we traded our pilgrim status for that of the tourist. Our commitment to God, man, and society is like the tourists' passing concern or mild curiosity about the problems of the foreign countries they visit, and we remain in fact uninvolved. Ours is a commitment circumscribed by the rational demands of convenience, not one dictated by the radicalism of the cross. The sad truth is that neither *The Wall Street Journal* nor the average churchman today can be labeled "as radical as the Christian doctrine." In the next chapter we need to expand further on the nature of radical faith.

III

The Nature of Radical Faith

One day Joe dropped by the office for a chat. Joe was a senior and a good student—the kind of person who contributes toward an instructor's own growth. I was glad he walked in.

"What's on your mind?" I asked. Joe looked rather pensive as he slumped into the easy chair and unfolded to me his increasing doubts about his Christian beliefs. The intensity and anxiety of his "confession" led to his searching cry, "I'm losing my faith!" Joe's concerns had been worrying him for some time. Joe, of course, is not alone. There are countless "Joes" in seminary, many reaching their senior year and harboring doubts which they refuse to reveal to fellow students and faculty.

The feeling of losing one's faith, while discussing the sacred materials of the faith, has always been a dangerous hazard in preparing for professional ministry. The phenomenon is not new; seminarians of yesteryear and those of today are confronted by the probing question, "What do I really believe?" *This is really the big question in life for everyone.* Since the seminarian has the opportunity to raise it with more intensity than most individuals, let's probe with him to understand the nature of radical faith.

Separating Faith from Theology

Each year's entering class of seminarians has varied during my decade plus of seminary teaching. One factor, however, remains the same: namely, the large number of students who have made no distinction between faith and theology. The confusion in this area has caused more than one student to reach the senior year and then realize that he has refused an education. How to go through seminary without learning is almost the hidden wish of some students who are actually afraid that the seminary process (a necessary means to obtain one's union card) will undermine their "faith." Not infrequently a seminarian will share with me the fact that a pastoral friend, a grandfather, or a saintly mother offered the parting advice, "Now, don't you let any seminary take away your faith!" *Substitute "learning" for "seminary" and the foregoing statement could apply to all of us.* The treasured relationship with a particular friend or relative who has implanted that type of advice often engenders an implicit, if not explicit, suspicion of the faculty, the seminary, and all new ideas.

My own experience includes many believers with "clenched fists" defying the professor to take away their "faith." Without sufficient awareness of this factor, the instructor and the student can spend a whole semester bypassing each other through showers of verbiage. The instructor must depart from his own agenda and begin to construct a bridge of understanding by identifying and recognizing the "faith" which each student has and protects with his (or her) clenched fist.

This necessary process of identifying one's faith will facilitate fruitful dialogue where theologizing can flourish to the mutual enrichment of student and instructor. Often as the student shares his faith with his fellow students in the classroom, a valuable informational and supportive climate results. Slowly, one begins to see the clenched fists relax to open palms signifying a more receptive spirit to learning. Has this been true in your experience, whatever your field of interest?

Inevitably, the transition from fist to palm helps anyone to make an appreciative and also critical appraisal of the sources which have nurtured his faith to date. Without denying the vitality of previous experiences or the trust placed in him by others, the student begins the slow but exciting process of identifying *The Source* beyond the sources. This is theologizing and is at the heart of the theological enterprise.

The faith of each student coming to seminary has been formulated and conditioned in numerous ways. For instance, the absence or presence of family devotions, grace at meal times, the testimony of a respected person or friend, and the desire to emulate that person, a "decision for Christ" at an evangelistic gathering, a dogmatic statement or confessional creed, Sunday worship services, etc. One could go on to list many other sources, or what I would prefer to call *theological casings.*

Let's take a careful look at all of these theological casings. The process of objectifying and identifying these casings can be rather painful for some—it may appear at times as an outright attack upon an individual's "faith." This may not be true at all in the effort to separate faith from theology. "Faith" maintained in a clenched fist may well be protection for a theological casing that is outmoded and inadequate. A student, like Joe, may not notice his "faith" slipping for lack of an adequate casing until late in his seminary career. Those students who have made the shift from fist to palm, hopefully, will become aware of the fact that they are not losing their "faith," but shedding outmoded wrappings that are blocking the stream of living faith flowing from the past to the future. The casing process, unwrapping and wrapping, is the theologizing activity necessary for the communication of a vital faith.

The Radicalness of Faith

Seminarians who feel that they are losing their "faith" often discover that they have been a parasite on someone else's struggle-filled pilgrimage. Consequently, some approach God in a second-hand manner. They come to God with borrowed crutches—theological casing which they have inherited or adopted. Should these borrowed crutches fail in a time of need, the feeling of losing one's "faith" becomes more pronounced. At times, this is accompanied by nostalgia for the comfortable past. Thus the student threatened by the loss of his adopted crutches desperately seeks some substitute crutch—something to satisfy his present needs.

In this pursuit from one set of crutches to the next, the pilgrim will begin to discover that living faith is communion with God without crutches. The call to come to God without crutches is so radical that we may refuse to accept the invitation, as we look frantically for some theological messiah to pull us through. Disappointment sets in when we discover how humanly limited all theological messiahs are. *There is really no escape from the radicalness of faith.* The truth is that God wants us to come to him without crutches of any kind. He alone is *The Source* worthy of our full commitment: "I am who I am. There is none other."

Until the priority of this claim is firmly fixed in our guts as well as our heads, we will go on losing our "faith" as the inadequacy of all theological casings, past and present, are pointed out to us wherever rigorous theologizing is maintained. True growth actually helps us to lose our theologies without losing our living faith in *The Source.* Philosopher Alfred North Whitehead perceptively stated that "religions commit suicide when they find their inspiration in their dogmas." This is true for Christianity, and Whitehead's definition of religion as "the denunciation of gods" can be appreciated. If we are negligent in questioning the theological "gods" in the marketplace, we are shirking our responsibility to identify, articulate, and nurture faith in the living God.

A Pilgrim Theology

As a community, we must recover the Biblical radicalness of faith that lies behind our distrust of structures, theological labels, and their limitations. In light of the Letter to the Hebrews we must recapture our focus on faith as "the assurance of things hoped for, the conviction of things not seen." A faith in the living God must be reasserted within our theologies. Nicolas Berdyaev, the Russian philosopher, writes:

> Theological doctrine is not necessary for faith, but faith is necessary for theological doctrine. And this means a primacy is given to spiritual experience over theological doctrine and that the true theology is the theology of spiritual experience.

(For further insights into his thoughts see my work on *Berdyaev's Philosophy of Hope,* Augsburg Publishing House, 1969.) In short, our spiritual experiences are not fully covered by explanations; our questions outnumber our answers. These are aspects of the unresolved tension between mystery and meaning. This is the nature of a pilgrim's theology.

Our wish to have answers for all our questions has tempted us to subvert our traditional theologies into crutches in our relationship to the living God. The truth is that God is beyond our grasp. The desire for an authoritative faith in our respective traditions has too often been a rationalizing attempt to "corner" God. "Let God be God" has been the reforming spirit of the church in every age. This spirit must be reaffirmed again and again to avoid entrapment in parochialism or the latest fad.

Our theologizing must always include an awareness of our limitations. Theologian Gordon Kaufman of Harvard has delineated the limits in all "God-talk." (See *New Theology No. 4*, ed. Martin Marty and Dean Peerman, Macmillan, 1967.) When all is said and done, God is still incognito, beyond our grasp. Only through the Biblical revelation do we in faith worship a God of grace and mercy. For the Christian, this God is most meaningfully understood in Jesus Christ. Yet God in himself is unknowable; he is beyond our means for verification. At most, we can have only an attitude of reverent agnosticism regarding his inner nature.

The Eastern Orthodox tradition has long taught that God in his essence is unknown; only his energies can be discerned. This has been reflected in their apophatic method of negative theologizing, as opposed to our more positive or kataphatic theologizing in the West. (For a comparison of Eastern and Western approaches to theological foundations, see my work, *Icon and Pulpit: The Protestant-Orthodox Encounter,* The Westminster Press, 1968.) The Easternization of Christianity, resulting from our increased global awareness, will encourage us to place limits on theological conclusions.

We must remember to let God be God and to let Jesus be Jesus, rather than harmonize the two beyond our human knowledge and implications. We must allow the radicalness of faith, in the spirit of the Letter to the Hebrews, to permeate our witness as we communicate to others the simplicity of faith. Through private prayers, corporate worship, and the doxology we are reminded of the simplicity of our faith: the fact that our theological journey in this life is never completed. Ours is a pilgrim theology—of moving and of waiting—in response to the living Lord.

All the evidence is not in, and no matter how earnestly we try, the last word will be God's, not ours. This final (eschatological) reality is our line of accountability. Living on this side of that final line of accountability should humble us to limit our claims. We are reminded that all we say and do is within the shadow of his presence. It is our task then to question all existing theologies, prone as each is to the temptation of idolatry. By so doing, we will maintain the radicalness of our faith. H. Richard Niebuhr in his book *The Meaning of Revelation* (p. 77, Macmillan, 1941), observed that "man as a practical, living being never exists without a god or gods; some things there are to which he must cling as the sources and goals of his activity, the centers of value." Continual honest probing is needed to help us distinguish among the gods, that our faith may be solidly anchored in the living God.

In over a decade of teaching, I have seen many students come to seminary and launch professional careers in the ministry. Hopefully, each has begun to grasp the significance of separating faith from theology, as we seek together the living God behind our theologies. Joe was not losing his faith, but rather deepening it—discarding theological casings he had brought to seminary. He had outgrown them, and the order of the day called for a new outfitting. In continuing his pilgrimage, he will be in need of further casings to embrace the enlarging breadth and depth of his faith in the living God. Such is the cutting nature of radical faith.

From Radicalness to Happiness

To speak of the radicalness of faith is a frightening prospect. After all, we are schooled most of our lives to exercise common sense and prudence. This, in part, explains why *The Wall Street Journal* is the gospel for so many. Its basic golden rule, "avoid illusions, be realistic" is the *Journal*'s corollary to common sense. Let Joe have his pilgrimage in seminary, but for the majority of us in the working world, the demand for security and happiness can't wait. We need to be satisfied *now.* Are these your feelings?

Are you searching for the source of happiness? There are those who would deny engaging in such a search. *Happiness* for them is a shallow term that speaks of cheap compromise. Others would readily admit engaging in the search, but confess, they haven't found happiness and seriously doubt if happiness can ever be found. Most are somewhere in between that vast spectrum, between the denial that we are searching and the doubt that we will find anything.

What is happiness? At a coffee break of faculty and students, the question of happiness came up. Some said, happiness is having a job, regaining a treasured object believed to be lost, being comfortable with yourself and with others, an event of significant importance—the birth of a child, hugging your wife, the ordination of a seminarian, catching a rainbow trout, and on the conversation went.

Returning home that day, I asked my family for their understanding of happiness. My twelve-year-old son replied—loving others and being loved, also getting a hit at the ball game. My fourteen-year-old daughter said, having a friend who sticks by you. Our seven-year-old daughter paused for a moment and then said, "Daddy, I want some ice cream." My wife indicated that happiness is "being appreciated." Being appreciated in tangible ways is certainly a deep need we all feel.

Turning to a group of married couples, the question of happiness elicited the following remarks: Happiness is peace of mind, reaching one's goal, influencing another person to accept your viewpoint. Happiness is turning forty and liking it, staying friends with your husband, starting a family, having a good conscience, receiving a letter from your son overseas. Happiness is having everything run smoothly at home and at work, seeing your children realize their potential in life, helping others in difficult situations, enjoying good health, serving a noble cause, and making up after a squabble.

Do these comments express the content of happiness for you? Have you found an answer that gives you satisfaction?

Does Money Buy Happiness?

Sometime ago United Press International reported the story of a New Jersey plumber who won a million dollars at a state-sponsored lottery contest. The newspaper carried a picture of the plumber grinning and crying at the same time; so overwhelmed was he with the news. The plumber was stunned to think that he would receive $50,000 a year from now until 1991. Catching his breath, he said, "I've been a plumber for twenty-four years and I'm tired of it, cleaning out sewers and doing things like that for $141.00 a week take home pay, while my wife works nights to help pay the bills. Those days are now over." Would that be happiness for you—to win a million dollars?

Would a sufficient amount of money solve your problems?

Richard A. Easterlin, Professor of Economics at the Wharton School of Finance and Commerce, University of Pennsylvania, writes in *The Public Interest* (Winter, 1973) an article entitled, "Does money buy happiness?" In it he states that "each person acts on the assumption that more money will bring more happiness; and, indeed, if he does get more money, and others do not (or get less), his happiness increases." But Professor Easterlin hastens to add that "when everyone acts on this assumption and incomes generally increase, no one, on the average, feels better off." The sad conclusion he draws is that "each person goes on, generation after generation, unaware of the self-defeating process in which he is caught up."

Another question he considers is whether increased incomes for all will increase happiness for all. Will a general rise in the standard of living enhance happiness within society? His findings are the following:

> *In all societies, more money for the individual typically means more individual happiness. However, raising the incomes of all does not increase the happiness of all.* The happiness-income relation provides a classic example of the logical fallacy of composition—*what is true for the individual is not true for society as a whole.*

Professor Easterlin's studies indicate that happiness is not the result of material well-being, but rather of being one step above one's surroundings no matter what the level. I would assume that this "happiness" would be very short-lived since usual practice indicates that our surroundings would quickly catch up or we would seek higher surroundings.

Easterlin again mentions three factors which seem prominent in shaping happiness—economics, family considerations, and health. "In all cultures the way in which most adults spend most of their time is the same—working, trying to provide for and raise a family, dealing with family problems and sickness." Given this cycle, data on the comparative happiness of income groups within a country indicates on the average that higher-income people are happier than the poor. This does not mean, however, that there are no unhappy people among the rich and no happy people among the poor.

For instance, writes Easterlin,

> in a December 1970 survey of the American population, not much more than a fourth of those in the lowest income group (under $3,000 annual income) reported that they were "very happy." In the highest income group identified in the survey (over $15,000) the proportion that was "very happy" was almost twice as great. In successive income groups from low to high, the proportion "very happy" rose steadily. For the typical individual, it would seem, more money brings with it more happiness.

According to the Census Bureau's report on American marriage patterns conducted in 1971, it was found that

> for households whose heads are from 35 to 54 years old, higher income and more schooling were associated with greater family stablity. Among families earning under $5,000 a year, 71.7 per cent had been married just once. This first-marriage figure rises steadily with income level, and for families earning $15,000 or more, fully 83.0 percent of husbands and wives were found to be in their first marriage. (Public Interest, p. 135.)

These findings may indicate some correlation between income and happiness, although not necessarily a cause and effect relationship.

Turning to *The Great Ideas: A Syntopicon of Great Books of the Western World,* (Vol. I, pp. 684-693) edited by Mortimer J. Adler, the topic of happiness receives extensive comment by many of the famous thinkers of the past. There is no doubt that mankind throughout the centuries has desired happiness. "'Man wishes to be happy,'" wrote Pascal, "'and only wishes to be happy, and cannot wish not to be so.'" According to Kant, happiness consists in "'the satisfaction of all our desires: *extensive,* in regard to their multiplicity; *intensive,* in regard to their degree; and *protensive,* in regard to their duration.'" For Aristotle, the most outstanding characteristic of the happy man is that he wants for nothing. He is content with his lot. This caused Boethius to say that happiness is "'a life made perfect by the possession in aggregate of all good things.'" From this standpoint, happiness is not a particular good in itself, but the sum of goods.

For Plato, happiness was identified with spiritual well-being. There needs to exist a harmony from a proper ordering of all the soul's parts resulting in an inner peace. Socrates expressed it well in the *Republic,* by stating that the just man " 'sets in order his own inner life, and is his own master and his own law, and is at peace with himself.' " Aristotle would concur with this, for happiness is activity in accordance with virtue.

St. Thomas Aquinas added that " '*happy is the man who has all he desires, or whose every wish is fulfilled.*' " Lockĕ reinforced this thought: " 'Happiness is the utmost pleasure we are capable of' "; and for Mill happiness is " 'an existence exempt as far as possible from pain, and as rich as possible in enjoyment.' " In contrast to these comments, Pierre Bezùkhov in *War and Peace* learned through his bitter experiences that " 'man is created for happiness; that happiness lies in himself, in the satisfaction of his natural human cravings; that all unhappiness arises not from privation but from superfluity.' " There is here the strong suggestion that if we externalize happiness that it will be nothing less than an illusory goal. How many of us have fallen into this trap? As affluent Americans, how often have we been obsessed with happy endings defined in material terms? On the other hand, to be told that goods are empty and that we should concentrate on the internal essentials of life may sound as hollow rhetoric if we are living a jobless and faceless existence in our community.

In retrospect, *The Great Ideas* suggests that "happiness is the quality of a whole life, not the feeling of satisfaction for a moment." Happiness consists of external and internal essentials. The latter is not always easy to define, but indicative of the fact that the passing moments of our earthly life are a pilgrimage. As long as life goes on, happiness is something to be pursued rather than fully possessed or enjoyed. There is no doubt that everyone wants happiness, but to what extent we are to internalize or externalize our pilgrimage will depend upon our particular frame of reference and faith. Economic considerations alone do not promise the full measure of happiness.

Yet, the findings of Professor Easterlin cannot be easily dismissed. The fact that the happiness-income relation for the individual does not correspond for the society as a whole must be pondered further. It implies that the way a society perceives its needs does not necessarily coincide with individual perceptions. "The satisfaction one gets from his material situation," writes Easterlin, "depends not on the absolute amount of goods he has, but on how this amount compares with what he thinks he needs." What the individual thinks he needs, of course,

> is socially determined, and those who live in richer times and places perceive their needs in more ambitious terms than those in poorer societies. Needs, or material aspirations, are formed as the result of prior and on-going experience in a society—in the language of sociology, through the socialization experience of the individual. Thus what one "needs" as he reaches adulthood typically depends on the impressions he has formed of "how to live" from observing life around him and in his society while growing up. *(ibid.)*

If this is true, then we are directed to the uncomfortable observation that perhaps we are indeed trapped in a material rat-race, hooked on what has been described as a "hedonic treadmill." While our economic growth continues to produce an even more affluent society, those of us caught in the process might well find that the very affluence we are aspiring to will always remain elusive, only to find it exposed someday as the Wizard of Oz who had a reputation of spectacular promise but no power to support his rhetoric.

We all need some fiction to live by; life without fiction could be unbearable. The Wizard of Oz isn't alone. I suspect that even the *Journal*'s own golden rule ("avoid illusions, be realistic") is tainted with fiction. We all wish to report the realities of life objectively, but our biases do get in the way. To aim for reality might well be our goal, but our perceptions of reality are at best approximations of its totality. I will discuss this point in fuller detail in a later chapter. For now, I wish to underscore the value of fiction. It should never be underrated.

The next time you view a movie, read a novel, or relate a story to children, pause to reflect on the value of fiction in daily life. Most of us need some fiction to flavor our lives; the question is always, "How much?" When does fiction crowd out the realities and tend to produce complete illusions? When does the *Journal* itself slip into this practice and fall short of its own motto for realism?

In fact, we all use fictional aids to cover up the realities of our appearances—women with their cosmetics and men with their smooth shaves. Our society accepts this, for one's public appearance is given high priority. Most of us prepare ourselves for the public from the moment we awake in the morning. The question again is how much fiction does society allow a person to accept and to practice? When does society judge a person too far into the fictional realm and thus a psychotic in need of care? How much *living fiction* can you and I absorb in a day? Our answer to these questions will help us to scrutinize our perceptions, to be more consciously aware of our private filter systems—a mysterious mixture of fact and fiction.

The Simplicity of Happiness

A class of fifth grade boys and girls at school sang a song entitled "Happiness" written by Clark Gesner. The lyrics describe happiness as having two flavors of ice cream, finding a lost key, learning to tell time or tie a shoe. Other pictures of happiness are knowing a secret, finding a nickel (it was a penny years ago), sharing a sandwich, enjoying morning and evening. The song ends with the thought that whoever and whatever we love is our happiness.

We could all add to these suggestions of happiness with many simple and satisfying experiences, yet the pursuit for happiness continues within us. Why? Perhaps we need to follow the example of the New York architect mentioned in the *Journal:* he found happiness when he threw out the telephone at home. The architect claimed this improved his life greatly. For a while, he admits, his teen-age daughter and son "really hated" him, but his wife was grateful. The arguments over whose turn it was at the telephone were driving the parents "batty." Now their children, when they tire of using the pay phone a few blocks away, visit friends and study more; and the daughter, with extra time on her hands, has even taken on a part-time job. Happiness is a new found silence at home.

In the business world today, some are finding that happiness means learning how to simplify their lives. A cartoon in the *Journal* illustrated a wife and her husband, a corporate executive, who was leaving home with a pack on his back. She implores, "But Rufus, a chairman of the board just can't say, 'I've had it,' and hit the road!"

Not long ago, the *Journal* reported in one of its front page stories, the example of Ross Denver, age 52, who quit a $50,000-a-year job as head of Amsted Industries Inc. Today this business executive tills a cranberry bog in Three Lakes, Wisconsin, and his wife keeps the books. "I have a lot of suits and shoes I'll never use again," he says with a smile and without regrets. No doubt simplifying one's life in an age of complexity and excessive pressure certainly does bring a measure of relief and happiness.

Most people, however, are not making $50,000 and may not be able to afford the simplicity of leaving their jobs. This is probably the situation for you. The point, however, isn't how much you earn, but whether your job is a source of happiness or unhappiness for you. Do you find yourself existing from one coffee break to the next? Are your best times after work, while hating the hours at your job? If your answers are in the affirmative, then you need to simplify your life, rearrange your priorities; for life is too short and too sweet to spend the best part of each day wishing you were somewhere else.

What then has our search for happiness revealed? Namely, that there are numerous labels given to happiness, and that no single label sums up accurately the content of happiness. *The beginning of maturity is to discover that happiness is an evasive quality. The source of happiness is actually beyond our grasp.* Any source in your grasp will turn out to be no more than a passing fancy, and you will go on with your relentless search.

Frankly, if we were to sum up all the responses to happiness, *the source* of happiness would still remain incognito. Happiness is more than persons, important as it is to find trusting friendships. Happiness is more than satisfying our material needs for security, in spite of our needs for the goods of life. Happiness is more than serving worthy institutions and causes, necessary as they are. Happiness is more than peace of mind, for there are storms in life which make our little canoes look pretty silly. The clue to happiness extends beyond persons, things, causes, institutions and peace-of-mind cults.

Where then is happiness to be found? *It is centered in the living God.* It really involves *the big question* (belief in God) that Joe, the seminarian, was raising. *Happiness is a gift from him.* Happiness is not dependent upon the beguiling gods of fellowship, worthy causes, institutions, or charismatic figures who can promise much, but fail to satisfy. To misplace your ultimate trust in anything or anyone less than the living God is to disappoint yourself. The Biblical witness is clear on this score—the happy person is one who trusts in the LORD. (Proverbs 16:20)

The wisdom of Proverbs is very contemporary. It informs us that the nature of happiness has a transcendent dimension. Happiness is commitment to the living Lord, not a commitment to the many gods of momentary happiness we encounter during our lifetime.

The individual who engages God in prayerful conversation is the truly happy person. But, oftentimes, we make no attempt to devotional books, trusted sayings, monetary sessions, close friends, etc. Happiness, however, is coming to God directly with complete trust. Happiness is really another name for faith. Happiness, like faith, involves utter trust in God. The demand is so radical that we refuse to believe it. The fact is that we can never escape the radical nature of faith.

God alone is worthy of our full commitment. Only God satisfies our thirst for happiness. As we accept the radicalness of our faith, we will free ourselves from the limitations of common sense in exchange for the wisdom and power of God. The next chapter will take a closer look at the pitfalls facing the *Journal*'s readers and their world.

IV

The Reader's World

The headline on the front page of *The Wall Street Journal* (March 29, 1974) read—**"Many People's Dreams Came Crashing Down With Equity Funding**—Widow May Need Welfare, Bachelor Is Distraught, Sick Man Keeps Working—'How Can I Tell My Wife?'" The story written by William Blundell of the *Journal*'s staff describes the effects of the Equity Funding scandal on its investors. This was one of several stories on the company reported by the *Journal* since the scandal—a stock whose market value a short time ago was about $288 million and today is worth nothing.

The losses from Equity Funding, one of the biggest and most audacious security frauds in history, hit the small investors the most. "For them, Equity Funding means a pinched household budget, a vacation untaken, a new home still a dream, wearing old clothes because they can't buy new ones, or a blighted retirement. There is much bitterness." One 30-year-old bachelor from Sherman Oaks, California, had most of his savings ($22,500) tied up in the company. He expressed the feelings of many, saying, "'I've had to pound and grind to make that. I can't count the nights I've sat up sighing and saying to myself, "Everything you worked for for years is gone."'" This same bachelor reported that after brooding over the newspaper accounts, "he found himself getting stomach pains at the very sight of *The Wall Street Journal* and had to stop reading it altogether for a while. But another victim, Lydia Bowe, says that the 'whole thing was like a novel, fascinating,' and has a scrapbook several inches thick filled with clippings." Equity Funding is one example among others that alerts the reader to the realities of this imperfect world.

Existing but not Living:

Another harsh reality in the reader's world today is the experience of inflation. The *Journal* has had many articles on this subject, including a series on "The Cost of Living." The descriptive headlines touch upon a cross-section of American lives:

> **For a Welfare Family, Inflation Has Meat Cutting into the Bone**—Existence of Claire Steere and Her Three Children Gets Harder & Harder (May 21, 1974)
>
> **With $5,684 a Year, Retired Couple's Life is a Test of Endurance**—Henry and Gertrude Harff, Beset by Rising Prices, Survive by Being Frugal (June 3, 1974)
>
> **Easy Street Eludes One Career Woman Making $9,200 a Year**—Spending More for Basics, New Yorker Jill Weber Can Afford Few Splurges (May 14, 1974)
>
> **A Young Couple Finds Life Has Few Frills on a $12,000 Salary**—Tom and Linda Moore Wage 'A Never-Ending Battle' Against Soaring Prices (May 6, 1974)
>
> **Family With $22,000 a Year Is Squeezed by College Expenses**—With Three to Educate, Chuck and Marty Douds Have One Goal: Saving (May 28, 1974)
>
> **Even Millionaires Are Airing Complaints About Rising Prices**—Despite Cushion of Wealth, Don and Alice Ingram See Need to Cut Corners (June 12, 1974).

The impact of the series makes it evident that skyrocketing consumer prices are being felt in almost every household. Beyond this material side of survival is the underlying question—survival to what end? The limitation of personal funds raises the issue of priorities and values in life. Are we Americans (whatever our income or lack of it) so absorbed in squeezing out a living that we are only existing?

This question also faces us from the energy crisis and the limitations of our natural resources. Professor Amitai W. Etzioni of Columbia University was quoted extensively by James P. Gannon of the *Journal*'s staff in an article entitled, "Getting Off the Treadmill" (April 12, 1974). Professor Etzioni detects "a creeping erosion of commitment to the earning-spending ethic" of Americans. We are gradually getting tired of just existing—"working hard and consuming hard"—but not really experiencing the joy of living. We seem to be questioning our central aim in life, which has been "the production of resources during working-hours and the consumption and destruction of them in leisure time." What we are witnessing is "the executive who stops taking home a briefcase full of work on weekends," or the factory worker who wants to work less overtime and "take early retirement at age 62" or earlier, or the young father with a household of three children earning an income of $14,356 a year and confessing, "I know I'm living above my income level. And I know I'm wasting my life away working. It's asinine. But it's the American way."

Today, we are having second thoughts on "the American way." To make a living is no longer enough for us; work also has to make a life. We are interested now in working to live rather than just living to work. We seem to be shifting from the "Protestant ethic" of hard work and thrift. The fact is that senior citizens who can afford to live in the "leisure world" of their choice are enjoying "fun and games" today without guilt. Many of them wonder why they wasted their youth—struggling so hard to scrimp and save; they were only existing for most of their lives. They are trying desperately now to recover "lost time" in their sunset years.

Of course, this kind of hedonistic outlook on life could be self-destructive to our society as it was for Rome in its heyday. The emphasis upon living, not merely existing, should point to a quality of life that goes beyond "eating, drinking, and being merry." Nonetheless, Professor Etzioni's observation that Americans are "getting off the treadmill" and losing interest in a life-style of simply "working hard and consuming hard" merits our attention.

As society shifts from work and consumption, it will spend more of its energies not only on pleasure activities but also artistic pursuits, preoccupation with sensitivity groups for personal and interpersonal growth, and greater involvement with public affairs and the political process through old-fashioned town meetings, seminars, and workshops.

This growing phenomenon of Americans jumping off the "accelerating production–consumption treadmill" was revealed to me through a round of interviews over a period of time in preparation for this book. I spent time in various industries, talked to countless businessmen, managers, professionals, and homemakers, and consulted many seminarians who come from amazingly diverse backgrounds and job experiences.

One day, I was talking with the proprietor of a small business in one of our larger Eastern cities. As I entered the store, I noticed a sign announcing that he would soon be closed for a two-week vacation. "How can you afford to be closed?" I asked. "Aren't you afraid that you will lose your customers to your competition? Won't people lose the habit of coming to your grocery store during a two-week absence?"

"Well," he said, "it's the chance I take, but it's worth it. My father never took off a day in his life when he ran the store, and now he's an old man too tired to enjoy life. Not me, I want to live! I have learned to cut costs, limit my expansion, my consumption, and in general trade off greater income for a more rounded and enriched life."

He also added, "I play the violin and take it seriously; I have also taken lessons in karate and am now enrolled at learning massage. For our vacation, my wife and I will spend a week attending summer concerts and another week with a sensitivity-group in a nudist camp."

Getting off the treadmill will become the life-style of many as the number of extended weekends increases. Millions of Americans will seek ways to enhance their quality of life no longer satisfied to be numbered statistically the 6% of the world's population consuming one-third of the world's energy, and yet not really living.

We are fast becoming what author Peter Schrag in *The New York Times* calls a "post-achievement" society.

> [Our] country has outrun the achievement ethic and the premises of growth. But we have yet to develop a post-achievement ethic that tries to deal with the likelihood that henceforth everything will be limited: resources, space, time and the kind of social mobility that the country has associated with geographical or technological frontiers. ("The Tunnel at the End of the Light," January 16, 1974.)

According to Schrag, the forthcoming post-achievement ethic will involve fundamental social and psychological changes, recognizing "the need for a base of civility and common services, and the inherent danger of an achievement rhetoric in which people have ceased to believe." Such an ethic will also admit the declining marginal satisfaction that the affluent derive from additional goods and services.

In short, progress need no longer be considered the iron law of American history as it has for the past two hundred years. We have arrived; we have achieved enormous material accomplishments. The emphasis in the future, in a post-achievement culture, will be upon the improvement of the general quality of life for the whole society, with the accent upon living rather than *existing*. What it means to live well will depend, of course, upon your priorities and values, which in turn depend upon your faith assumptions in life.

Whom Can You Trust?

While some readers of the *Journal* are no longer waiting until they reach the mythical line of retirement to enjoy life, they are faced with the dilemma of whom to trust in their day–to–day battles for self-fulfillment and dignity. Gone, it seems, are the old-fashioned "gentlemen's agreements" based upon truth and mutual respect. Our lives have become too complex; communication among individuals is multi-dimensional. Eye-ball to eye-ball contact and the simple handshake are still practiced in some quarters, but for the most part, collective bargaining and technical legal documents are the normal style–of–life in our urbanized business culture.

There is always the nostalgic longing for the "good-old-days," and some churches continue to preserve the myths of yesterday which no longer apply in Monday's world. The astute parishioner who picks up his *Journal* during the week and reads that "Jim Williams' **Career as a Corporate Chief Ended in a Prison Cell**—Westec Corp.'s Ex-Chief Got 15 Years for Stock Fraud; Lost: a Wife, a Reputation" (October 3, 1972), knows that the notion of trust is badly shaken today. The Williams story was actually a part of a longer series of articles published by the *Journal,* illustrating "successful" men who had reached the heights of corporate life, but subsequently lost their position of trust and leadership.

The notion of trust has been proclaimed as an essential part of our business creed. (See *The American Business Creed*, by Francis X. Sutton, Seymour E. Harris, Carl Kaysen, and James Tobin, Harvard University Press, 1956.) Max Weber in his celebrated study, *The Protestant Ethic and the Spirit of Capitalism* (Charles Scribner's Sons, 1958), shows that businessmen believed that they were called to work for the greater glory of God. This in turn implied high standards of excellence and of honesty in all business practices. This emphasis upon their high calling provided the basis of trust for businessmen, among themselves and with consumers.

Today, we continue to give lip service to this business creed which has minimum correlation with our daily practices. In the course of my interviews, one industrial executive spoke bluntly, "Everybody is in business to make money. . . . There's no trust when things are tight . . . When things are going well, people are generous." He also added, "Sure, there's a need for some measure of trust . . . but collateral is the basis for any credit. The days of gentlemen's agreements are over. . . ."

Another manager, on discovering that I was a theologian studying business practices, took me aside for some lessons in the hard realities of life. "Do you know," he said, "that in life you must go out to win—if you want to be a loser, then be a 'good guy' like teachers, ministers, and social workers."

He also felt that trust is a luxury in our world. Once the trust placed in someone is destroyed, you are the loser. "When you learn how to lose," he said, "you learn to compensate a loss with a win. Losses are an education; winning is your diploma. As for myself, I don't believe in losses; I make winners out of everyone."

The manager that I was interviewing was, by the way, an active churchgoer, but he had long ago decided that Sunday and Monday were two different worlds. To try to integrate them would be an exercise in futility. "In fact," he said, "if you ask me how to be a Christian in business, my answer is that you can't, or you won't survive. Any book on the topic would be the shortest on record."

Perhaps this business executive is more of a cynic than a realist, and we might want to discount his outlook. On the other hand, as Americans with an optimistic bent, we may be terribly naïve about the subtlety and intrigue of daily life. We like to keep our interpretation of life simple. However, realities indicate a complex world where the average citizen is finding it more difficult than ever to trust anyone.

Irving Kristol, Professor of Urban Values at New York University and a member of the *Journal*'s *Board of Contributors,* writes a penetrating article for the *Journal* entitled "The Credibility of Corporations." Professor Kristol states that the problem facing our business corporations

> is one of candor and credibility, not—repeat: not—of "public relations." Indeed, one of the reasons the large corporations find it so difficult to persuade the public of anything is that the public always suspects them of engaging in clever public relations, instead of simply telling the truth.

Professor Kristol feels strongly that "the reason the public is so suspicious is because our large corporations so habitually do engage in clever public relations instead of simply telling the truth." (January 17, 1974.) The trust factor is so basic to our organization of life, yet so widely abandoned today! How can trust be regained? How can we seek to turn our society into a cohesive fabric? How can the threads of complexity be interwoven to shed light on our contemporary problems? These are the crucial questions today. The sad fact is that we lack any unifying ethics to meet the obligation set before us.

U. S. News & World Report, in a special section (February 25, 1974), reported on "How America Is Changing." The account shared the findings of a study conducted by Louis Harris & Associates, Inc., for the U.S. Senate Subcommittee on Intergovernmental Relations, and reported that, with few exceptions, confidence in major institutions has decreased sharply since 1966.

> For institutions of higher education, the decline is from a confidence level of 61 per cent in 1966 to 44 per cent last year. Confidence in the executive branch of government fell from 41 to 19 per cent; in the U.S. Supreme Court from 51 to 33 per cent; in major companies, from 55 to 29 per cent.

What the Harris poll and others are saying is that Americans are "increasingly distrustful of churchmen, scientists, businessmen and bureaucrats. Court and legislative hearings over charges of presidential involvement in financial 'deals' and political espionage stir responses ranging from disbelief to cynicism—a 'crisis of disbelief' in a nation whose hallmark not too long ago was optimism." Whom can you trust is no small issue in a society of lonely crowds in search of authentic human relationships.

What comfort is the *Journal*'s gospel in this environment? To implement the *Journal*'s golden rule—avoid illusions, be realistic—makes good sense in a business transaction, but what about our needs for intimacy, our longings for genuine fellowship and warm human affection in a community of kindred spirits? Are hippie communes and sensitivity groups the only alternatives where trusting relationships can be experienced at least sporadically?

The *Journal* is well aware of the human predicament, but it doesn't offer any answers to our questions. The *Journal* captures our moods and feelings in such feature stories as the one describing bartender, John Gallagher, whose work involves much more than mixing martinis. N. R. Kleinfield of the *Journal* staff writes (January 22, 1973) that Gallagher also dispenses advice, help, even loans to regulars at Costello's bar on Third Avenue near 44th Street in New York City.

> The problems of his patrons are often mundane: what model car to purchase, whether a daughter is old enough to accept a date. But sometimes they are as severe as the loss of a job or a wife. "You're like a chaplain hearing confession 10 hours a day," the bartender says. "You have to have all the answers. I just try to be patient and comforting. I don't kid myself that I can solve all the world's problems. But I give it a try."

In a society of strangers afraid to trust each other, the bartender is man's best friend for some customers.

Today, a new common practice is to find chaplains assisting at our larger motels. Holiday Inns, Inc., now have a chaplain on call in 1,331 of the chain's 1,638 motels, according to the *Journal*'s staff reporter Ron Cooper (May 21, 1974). The average motel chaplain gets about 15 calls a year; some receive less, others many more. Not knowing whom to trust, motels are natural refuges for the troubled. "When people are running away from something, they run to a neutral place," according to the Rev. Jack Chellew, one of Holiday Inn's numerous chaplains on call. Individuals are looking for someone to confide in, and the relative anonymity of the chaplain-on-call program is much more appealing than talking with your own pastor.

Others, if not running to an anonymous third party to confide in, turn on television for relief as they vision the simple and wholesome family life of "The Waltons." In our fantasy, we at times think that trusting relationships can be found if we could turn the clock back to simpler times. Others of us may want to change our place of residence. Take for instance, the small town in Appleton, Iowa, where George Apple and his wife, four children, his father, three dogs, a horse, a snake, and six hamsters live since their move from the hustle and bustle of California. The fictional story was told in a charming way on the television program known as "Apple's Way."

The loving and trusting relationship found in "Apple's Way" is a longing for a reality that's not there, as Benjamin Stein states so well in the *Journal* review article entitled "Is Iowa All That Wholesome?" (April 1, 1974.) And yet, Christopher Morley has a point when he says, "Every man needs to have an apple orchard tucked away in his heart—a someplace to contemplate, to anticipate—even if he never tastes the apples." We do need our moments of quiet retreat, and that can take place anywhere.

Having spent most of my life in California, and more recently many years in Iowa, I found that trusting relationships are not a matter of geographic location. Such trust is actually found where individuals are willing to take on the responsible risks involved in being open with each other. Given our society, given our present attitudes on life, how many of us can afford to risk such openness?

The Drive for Status and Security

Whether we can afford to be open or not will be determined by our needs for status and security. These concerns are vital to the *Journal*'s readership. The twin drives for status and security are integrally interrelated—it is difficult to say which comes first, even as we keep in mind Abraham H. Maslow's hierarchy of needs. (See his book *Motivation & Personality*, Harper Bros., 1954.)* Both drives

*Other important works on theories of motivation are: Elton Mayo, *The Human Problems of an Industrial Civilization,* Macmillan, 1933; Kurt Lewin, *Field Theory in Social Science,* Harper & Row, 1951; Douglas McGregor, *The Human Side of Enterprise,* McGraw-Hill, 1960; Chris Argyris, *Integrating the Individual and the Organization,* John Wiley & Sons, 1964; Rensis Likert, *New Patterns in Management,* McGraw-Hill, 1961; Robert R. Blake and Jane S. Mouton, *The Managerial Grid,* Gulf Publishing Co., 1964; and Frederick Herzberg, *Work and the Nature of Man,* World Publishing Co., 1966.

are basic contributors to an individual's self-esteem and survival. Our drives for status and security have been largely conditions which Harry Levinson, formerly of the Harvard Business School and President of the Levinson Institute, has described as "the great jackass fallacy." The great jackass fallacy is the carrot-and-stick philosophy of reward and punishment practiced in our business culture. It is the most dominant philosophy of motivation in American management today.

Mr. Levinson is critical of this philosophy, as it undermines the status and security of the employee and along with it his self-esteem and survival in the organization. According to Levinson,

> as long as anyone in a leadership role operates with reward-punishment assumptions about motivation, he is implicitly assuming that he has (or should have) control over others and that they are in a jackass position with respect to him. Such a relationship is inevitably one of condescending contempt whose most blatant mask is paternalism. (*The Great Jackass Fallacy,* p. 11, Harvard University Graduate School of Business, Division of Research, 1973.)

The result of such practices is an endless battle between those who seek to wield power and those who are subject to it.

How then are we to satisfy our needs for status and security and not at the same time be victimized by the carrot-and-stick philosophy? The *Journal*'s prescription to its readers—avoid illusions, be realistic—applies here to the issues of status and security. The *Journal* never promises a "rose garden"—everyone will not enjoy the same status or have the same measure of security. To think outherwise is to be unrealistic and the victim of illusion. We must learn to accept our imperfect world; society will always consist of winners and losers. The wide variety of feature stories that appear on the *Journal*'s front page describes individuals in both columns—winners and losers. This is the human scene for the *Journal.*

There is, for example, the story of realty agent Joan Thomas, written by Roger May (May 20, 1974) of the *Journal,* describing a successful 45-year-old divorcée with five children who range in age from eleven to sixteen. Mrs. Thomas is a busy and successful agent;

she even spent last Mother's Day showing houses to out-of-towners. She sells on the order of twenty homes a year and has an approximate annual income of $30,000. In short, Mrs. Thomas is a winner and without doubt her story is an inspiration to countless women, especially those who are single-handedly responsible for the maintenance of their homes. No doubt she is paying a personal price for her success, but then hard work is an implicit aspect of reality in the *Journal*'s gospel.

Another illustration of optimism and hope was the feature story on Irving Shapiro, Du Pont's designated chief executive officer, written by Thomas Bray (December 14, 1973) of the *Journal*'s staff. Du Pont's Shapiro is Jewish, a Democrat, a lawyer (no lawyer has ever before broken into the higher echelons of Du Pont), a non-Du Pont, and an immigrant's son. What is important, however, is that the *Journal*'s readers know that Mr. Shapiro climbed up *the hard way*. Mr. Shapiro's rags-to-riches story is all the more remarkable considering the close-knit society associated with the Du Pont Company. Mr. Shapiro is a winner and his presence reinforces the American dream that ours is a land of opportunity.

An editorial in the *Journal* and other newspapers honored the accomplishment of Henry Aaron's surpassing of Babe Ruth's 39-year-old home run record ("Henry Aaron's Record," April 10, 1974). The editorial praised the ball player as an unobtrusive individual "who was content to let his bat and glove do his talking." Aaron's fame and place in baseball history is a demonstration in its own way "that almost nothing is out of reach for the person who combines perseverance with great talent." The editorial concluded that Aaron was not only an outstanding athlete but that his life-style was a worthwhile example for any man. Aaron indeed scores in the winner's column from the *Journal*'s perspective.

Often the heroes mentioned in the *Journal*'s articles have Midwest roots, like Deil O. Gustafson. The headline over his name describes him as an Iowa farm boy who now sits in the board room of the Tropicana Hotel and Casino in Las Vegas. "He also owns," reports Frederick C. Klein of the *Journal* (January 3, 1974), "the Carousel casino in downtown Las Vegas, banks, apartments, office buildings and large chunks of real estate in Minneapolis, a hotel in

Phoenix, a cattle ranch in northern Nevada and 20 or so companies engaged in selling insurance, leasing equipment, making movies and other things." According to Klein, the assets under his control exceed $150 million. "His net worth, which stood at close to zero in his teaching days, has been placed at $20 million to $30 million." Gustafson is definitely a winner for the *Journal* and its readers.

The Aarons, Gustafsons, Thomases, and Shapiros illustrate stories of hard–fought success. What about those who aren't making it in their climb for status and security? In a story under the heading, "Up-the-Ladder Blues," Liz Roman Gallese of the *Journal* (February 28, 1974), tells of white males who are unhappy that they are now victims of job discrimination. White males are voicing their anger that companies are favoring women and racial minorities in filling managerial posts. "'We found that white males are intensely angry—it's an Archie Bunker reaction, but it's real,' says James B. Webber, a director of Cambridge Research Institute Inc. in Massachusetts, who is studying this emerging phenomenon." This will become an increasing problem for those in their mid-thirties and forties who find themselves frustrated in their goals for status and security. White males with punctured self-esteem, fighting for survival, may give us second thoughts about dividing a society into winners and losers.

The *Journal* published an unusual series of articles under the theme, "The Nonworkers." The series involved eight individuals (appearing from February 9 to March 30, 1973 with a follow-up on September 11, 1973) who for various reasons were nonworkers. One was a nonworker married to wealth; others included a handicapped Vietnam veteran with shattered legs, a drunken bum with dreams of unfulfilled stardom, a young college graduate living on a neglected farm doing as little as possible to exist, a 56–year–old homemaker with an injured back who took care of the home while his wife worked, a 66–year–old retired engineer, a professional student with an M.D. among other degrees, and finally an unemployed welder struggling to find the proper job. What was the outcome of this series? It revealed the diverse circumstances in which individuals find themselves, and out of which they reshape their perspectives on life. Some of these "nonworkers" see themselves as losers, wasting their lives away, and still others are striving to survive meaningfully within our work-oriented society. I doubt if any of the individuals described see themselves as winners. The odds are that the category itself doesn't have any meaning for most of them. Will this tribe of nonworkers increase in the future? How will their increasing number affect our understanding of status and security?

In any reappraisal of our society, the values given to status and security will shape the character of that community. The *Journal*, sensing the need for a probing analysis, caught the mood of people in a perceptive article by Everett Groseclose. "Aimless America" (October 16, 1972) claims that the affluent, poor, old, and young are all turned inward trying to come to terms with their frustrations, restlessness, and increasing disenchantment with any optimistic vision for society. The reporter followed U.S. Highway 6 from Rhode Island to California, and found the mood of people he met possessed by a quiet desperation, disregarding the larger issues and preoccupied with only personal matters. People have come to question their own drives for status and security, as they come to realize that they are subject to larger institutions which are running the country. Such institutions are beyond the control of individuals, and yet their personal destinies are under the power of these institutions. People are feeling powerless. "'So people are just giving up. They're directing all their efforts toward influencing the things that, rightly or wrongly, they think they can control.'"

One high school principal met in Groseclose's travels felt that the most severe problem among recent high school graduates is apathy. Said the principal:

> "To these kids, the emptiness of graduation is very, very real. It means nothing to them. I keep telling them that they're right. It isn't so important to graduate from high school. What is important is to fit into our society as a useful and productive person. But it's all lost on them. I don't think we've got a single program in the U. S dealing effectively with this dissatisfaction, this aimlessness and alienation."

What will be our reaction to an emerging generation that is possibly non-status and non-security oriented? What new message of hope or possible threat will they present for us?

While we may resent aimless Americans in transition, we can at least be grateful that the younger generation is placing a higher price on their souls than we did. At times this tension is painfully seen between a father and a son, especially when the former counted on his son to follow and continue his foundations in business. Listen to Ben Davidson, a recent Harvard Business School graduate, in a conversation recorded by Peter Cohen (*The Gospel According to the Harvard Business School*, p. 324, Doubleday & Co., 1973). Mr. Davidson is reflecting upon the American business establishment and his own role and identity in relation to it:

> "I used to figure that if I wasn't happy with the milieu I was in, that was the price one pays; that you have to make some kind of sacrifice in terms of the people and the places, as it were. But I have found, over the last couple of months, that it takes a whole kind of psychology to exist in this world. Everyone is telling you a different story, based on *his* needs, *his* perspective, *his* own particular frame of reference. Everyone is protecting his own interests. It's a very hard world and, you know, why should I have to deal with this kind of people? Why should I have to become an overbearing manager? Because my father would like me to? Because that's the image of me he's got?"

Do we understand the concerns of Ben Davidson? *How much of ourselves have we disowned in order to be where we are today?*

"Attract, retain and motivate" is the standard operating goal among executive head-hunters. We live in a functionally oriented society where our sense of personhood and being are lost in the games that status seekers play. (See Robert Heller, *The Great Executive Dream,* Delacorte Publishing Co., 1972.) What about the growing number of persons who don't have any particular wish to achieve or to play the games that status and security demand? How will bosses handle them?

Can the Boss Be Human?

Ask the *Journal* this question—a large percentage of their readership is management. One *Journal* ad, "Noah's Ark on Madison Avenue," claimed that all the captains of industry read it: "The captains of chemicals and the captains of finance. The captains of aerospace and the captains of pharmaceuticals. The captains of metals, of fuels, of transportation, of foods. The captains of textiles and the captains of forest products. Of retailing. Of construction. Of every field that makes up the world of business." That's a lot of bosses!

Are these captains of business human? The obvious answer is *yes*. Yet, how often does the executive "play God" when making a personnel judgment or in a particular management crisis? Afterwards, he is quickly brought down to earth by realizing a stupid mistake or by the gentle prodding of his wife. Whatever the case, the captain is in a position of responsibility and influence. He has authority over the lives of others. He also needs the cooperation of others for smooth sailing if he wishes to deliver the promised cargo on time. In short, *the captains of management achieve their results by working through other people.*

Achieving results in more recent times has been referred to as "management by objectives" (MBO). The aim is to have a more rational management process where people know what they are to do, who is held accountable, and how compensation is to be related fairly to individual achievement. By laying bare the process, this method attempts to provide personnel with an opportunity to be self-motivating by setting their own objectives.

Mr. Harry Levinson has at this point raised an important question—management by whose objectives? He points out that

> Management by objectives and performance appraisal processes, as typically practiced, are inherently self-defeating over the long run because they are based on a reward-punishment psychology that serves to intensify the pressure on the individual while really giving him a very limited choice of objectives. (*The Great Jackass Fallacy,* p. 106.)

Management by objectives alone is another subtle form of manipulation by the boss, and consequently dehumanizes the workers. Such processes as management by objectives can be greatly improved, says Mr. Levinson, "by examining the psychological assumptions underlying them, by extending them to include group appraisal of superiors by subordinates, and by considering the personal goals of the individual first." This more comprehensive and ethical outlook will reveal the boss's humanity and concern for others. As a result, the entire morale of the organization would be enhanced.

Goals and a vision for creative future possibilities are important in any organization—industry, corporations, educational institutions, churches, etc. The executive who sees himself in partnership with others in reaching these goals will allow himself to be judged as well as judging the work of his fellow employees. How many employers will allow their employees to evaluate them and their performance? Perhaps such a practice is not in keeping with traditional management practice and complex labor relations through unions, but to change our ways might go far in improving the climate, attitudes, and performance of all concerned in the organization. This would also serve to keep the organization more human.

Major problems are quite often not with machines and materials, but with persons. The boss is usually most vulnerable in this area, and inadequacy here causes low morale. A news item in the *Journal* (May 29, 1973) highlighted the "White-Collar Blues" among management personnel:

> A survey of 2,821 executives shows an "alarming" 52% of supervisory managers "found their work, at best, unsatisfying." The American Management Association's study finds 30% of the executives believe business activities "have adversely affected their health in the last five years." Nearly 50% of them have changed, or have considered changing their occupational field since 1967.

People-problems are one of the major causes behind these "white-collar blues."

When employers and employees are in partnership, working toward mutually shared objectives, a healthier climate will prevail in that organization. In such a context, the manager can better raise questions and be concerned about qualitative aspects of performance. All parties concerned, acting together, can cope with issues without the barrier of being limited to statistics. Mr. Levinson indicates that the outcome will be a continuing process of interchange that would transcend static job descriptions and provide numerous avenues for feedback on performance and possibilities for new partnerships. The outcome would be a far more dynamic organization that is more personally satisfying and humane. It would also place more responsibility at the lower levels of the organization, freeing superiors "from the burden of the passed buck and the onus of being the purveyors of hostility." In such an organization, personnel would discover that their bosses are indeed human!

There are executives, of course, who would say that it's nonsense to think in terms of partnership; the name of the game is power, which resides with the chief executive officer and his subordinates. Robert N. McMurry of The McMurry Company, a firm of management psychologists and personnel consultants in Chicago, expresses this viewpoint in the *Harvard Business Review* (November-December, 1973) on "Power and the ambitious executive": "The most important and unyielding necessity of organizational life is not better communication, human relations, or employee participation, but power." He convincingly claims that

> without power there can be no authority; without authority, there can be no discipline; without discipline, there can be difficulty in maintaining order, system, and productivity. An executive without power is, therefore, all too often a figurehead—or worse, headless. The higher an executive is in his management hierarchy, the greater his need for power. This is because power tends to weaken as it is disseminated downward.

With the above position in mind, the boss's personal style, according to Mr. McMurry, is to be that of an executive-politician who (1) uses caution in taking counsel, (2) avoids too close superior-subordinate relationships, (3) maintains maneuverability, (4) uses passive resistance when necessary, (5) does not hesitate to be ruthless when expedient, (6) limits what is to be communicated, (7) recognizes that there are seldom any secrets in an organization, (8) never places too much dependence on a subordinate, (9) is willing to compromise on small matters, (10) is skilled in self-dramatization and is a persuasive personal salesman, (11) radiates self-confidence, (12) gives outward evidence of status, power, and material success, (13) avoids bureaucratic rigidity in interpreting company rules, (14) remembers to give praise as well as censure, and (15) is open-minded and receptive to opinions which differ from his. Mr. McMurry certainly touches upon many salient points in building his model for the ambitious executive, but is it human? It's certainly a model for efficiency, but is it too Machiavellian to create trust among personnel? One wise and retired chief executive officer in reviewing his own career said, "The best way to treat people is the Christian way . . . to have their interest at heart."

Author and corporate leader Robert Townsend refers to the boss's drive and humanity in an article entitled "The Ups and Downs of Working Life" in *The Center Magazine* (January-February, 1972). He says, "What any buisness needs as chief executive is anybody who will work full time at it, and who doesn't think he's a genius at anything." Mr. Townsend feels that it is important for the chief "to know the key people in each of his tribes, in addition to his key palace staff. Without trust in any organization there is little to build on. But trust is a by-product of justice. And how can he trust tribe leaders he does not know? How can they trust him?" The points made by Townsend are simple; yet how often by design the terrible distance between the chief and his tribe builds a wall of suspicion, resentment, elitism, and a faceless image of non-concern. The wise chief knows that all reality is based upon human rclationships. The mark of maturity in leadership is to recognize our interdependence upon each other. No one is exempt.

The boss who is interested in being human is concerned with maximizing profits and productivity, but also in maximizing the morale of his employees by fulfilling their basic needs. The executive with a future, states Harlan Cleveland in his book, *The Future Executive* (pp. 126-127, Harper & Row, 1972), will aim to meet modern man's four basic needs: (1) a sense of welfare—which includes a minimum standard of material goods agreed to by a consensus within that society, (2) a sense of equity—the individual's need to feel justly treated within his circumstances, (3) a sense of achievement—an individual's feeling that progress and movement is being made in some generally accepted direction, and (4) a sense of participation in deciding what those goals and directions will be. "What moves people to action," says Dr. Cleveland, "is more hope than fear, not just a vision of how bad things might become, but a vision of how things might be improved." (p. 86) Executives committed to enriching life for their employees will look beyond the boundaries of their own organization. John Gardner states that executives "'have to come out of the trenches of their own specialties and look at the whole battlefield.'"

It doesn't take long for a conscientious boss to find out how much is demanded of his time, energy, and emotions! A news report in the *Journal* (April 2, 1974) notes that despite the corporate executives' popular image as a high health risk, they

> enjoy a mortality rate only 63% of the rate for the general white male population, the Metropolitan Life Insurance Co. finds. Board chairmen picked from top companies on *Fortune*'s 500 list in 1957 had a 1972 death rate 69% of that for all white males. The study finds presidents in the group of 1,078 executives had an even lower rate, 58% of normal mortality.

Those in responsible positions, in spite of the pressures of their office, enjoy an above average level of physical and emotional fitness. Researchers find that work satisfaction and public recognition may be "an important determinant" of health and longevity. Those business leaders, I suspect, who share their responsibilities stand a better chance for a healthier life. Business leaders will never escape stressful situations and frustrating moments. Read, for example, the stories of corporate leaders written in *Dun's, Nation's Business, Business Week, Fortune,* etc. which illustrate along with the *Journal* that bosses were never promised a rose garden either.

One way for the boss to admit his own humanity to himself, is to acknowledge what he has accomplished. If his religious sensitivities are not asleep, he will also not forget to thank his God for life, health, and the opportunity to maximize his talents.

Before we conclude our discussion on the boss's humanity, let's not forget that in any organization

> dollars can be budgeted but human motivation can't. As a frame of reference in respect to funds available, budgets are essential. As a device for developing greater leadership, enthusiasm, dedication, reliability, cooperation, or for building the organization and improving its quality, budgets are a dull reflection of the machines used in their elaboration. (J. Douglas

Brown, *The Human Nature of Organizations,* p. 48, AMACOM, 1973.)

The sensitized boss will bear this in mind, as he practices both the science and the art of leadership. In doing so, he will give expression to his own humanity and to the humanity of others. He will also exercise optimum pace and timing for all decisions and actions that affect his employees and their larger environment. He will understand that, in the final analysis, people look to individuals for leadership, not committees. When such individuals are genuine human beings, not afraid to share their feelings and frailties along with their strengths and convictions, executives will have taken a real step forward.

In retrospect, we have seen some of the realities of the reader's world—fraud, inflation, trust, status, success, failure, security, the boss, and the organization—which are well covered in the *Journal.* In the next chapter, our discussion proceeds a step further—to the neglected side of the *Journal*'s gospel.

V

The Neglected Side of the *Journal*'s Gospel

In my conversations with members of the *Journal*'s staff, I was made aware of a critical article about the newspaper by a former staffer. The article was entitled "Up Against The Wall Street Journal" by A. Kent Macdougall (*MORE—A Journalism Review,* October, 1972) who was on the *Journal*'s staff for nearly a decade. The article exhibits mixed emotions—feelings of affection and resentment toward the *Journal.* It's not my purpose to espouse Macdougall's slanted perspective but to highlight an aspect of his criticism and test it out.

How Realistic Is the *Journal*?

Macdougall claims that the *Journal* "ignores the day-in, day-out systematic corruption that is built into the American way of doing business, the corporate corruption that is far greater and more pernicious than big city police corruption." He goes on to say that

> Ralph Nader and his associates have described how some businesses really do business. *The Wall Street Journal* rarely has. For all that many consider it the "Bible of Business," the *Journal* publishes more in-depth stories on medicine than on merchandising, more leaders on athletics than on agriculture, more on personalities than on petroleum.

Macdougall questions whether the *Journal,* as one of the finest newspapers of the land, fulfills its responsibility as a member of the fourth estate.

Basic to Macdougall's concern is the prior question: To what extent should the *Journal* set itself as the conscience of the business world? Macdougall believes the *Journal* should have this responsibility. Is the *Journal* raising its voice significantly in this area? "Taking on the biggest corporations, many of them practically countries unto themselves, is a lot tougher than going after the small fry that are the target of most investigative stories," according to Macdougall. In fact, Macdougall feels that the *Journal,* through a more rigorous program of business coverage, as well as non-business coverage, would win new readers as well as keep the old ones. "Nothing fascinates businessmen more than reading stories that embarrass other businessmen," says Macdougall. It has been Macdougall's experience that businessmen squawk "only when the rake reaches their own muck." Articles, however, should avoid, says Macdougall, "a crusading, muckraking tone; the paper's standard calm, matter-of-fact, balanced presentation is eminently serviceable." In short, as a specialized paper aimed primarily for the business community, the *Journal*'s content should include more business coverage, according to Macdougall, and especially reveal findings that may be critical of big business.

Is this a justified criticism of the *Journal*? My own observation indicates that it's exaggerated. I have found the *Journal*'s stories exposing big businesses as well as small frys. The *Journal* seeks to present a balanced job of reporting. Both quality and investigative skill have given the *Journal* a well deserved position of trust on the American scene. In 1974, for instance, the *Journal* won six awards for its reporting. The following were announced in the *Journal* (June 17, 1974) to its advertisers and readers:

• **The Overseas Press Club's award for best reporting on Latin America:** Won by Everett Martin for his outstanding coverage before, during and after the Chilean coup.

• **Scripps-Howard Foundation Public Service Award:** Won by Bill Lundell, the *Journal*'s Los Angeles bureau chief for his story that broke the Equity Funding Corporation scandal.

• **The Drew Pearson Award:** Won by Jerry Landauer for breaking the story about the inquiry into Spiro Agnew's finances and taxes.

• **The Meyer Berger Award, given annually by Columbia University:** Won by N. R. Kleinfield for his "handsomely styled stories on how New Yorkers live and work."

• **American Association for the Advancement of Science—**

Westinghouse Science Reporting Award: Won by David Brand for three *Journal* articles dealing with protein research, solar energy, and artificial intelligence.

- **The Howard Blakeslee Award of the American Heart Association:** Won by Jonathan Spivak for two articles; "Attacking a Killer" concerning steps being taken to reduce heart disease deaths; "Medical Debate" concerning the value and effectiveness of coronary bypass operations.

The above awards show a fair distribution of coverage among the numerous topics that appear in the *Journal.* Perhaps there could be some more critical business coverage, as Macdougall claims, but I don't consider this a serious defect in the *Journal.* Furthermore, it has been my observation that within the pages of the *Journal* there is an on-going dialectic between the news stories or articles which expose the practices of the establishment and the editorials which often defend the establishment.

It would be my contention that the *Journal* is fulfilling the press's role as the fourth estate and maintaining a high level of trust among its readership. Unlike Macdougall, I would contend that the *Journal* indeed espouses a crusading spirit within its pages. I'm sure that there are those on the staff who would deny it; they see their primary role as being descriptive rather than prescriptive. In fact, the *Journal* as a rule is generally suspicious of the "mentality of crusaders." Nonetheless, the *Journal*'s basic commitment which generates its crusading spirit is seen in its wish to uphold the mythical underpinnings of the establishment in a reasonable and enlightened way. This is clearly the case with the editorial page, where an interpretative outlook naturally is found. The *Journal*'s editorial page is crusading consistently for an implicit system of values, which might hold the answers to our contemporary problems. It is in these implicit values that I find the neglected side of the *Journal*'s gospel.

In other words, does the *Journal*'s implicit system of values reflect accurately the reader's world? Is the *Journal* an adequate compass to the complexity of our global island? Is the *Journal* faithful to its own golden rule—avoid illusions, be realistic? Is it possible that the implicit values are encased in myths which are now passé? Is the *Journal*'s leadership eclipsing the very realities which they feel duty-bound to expose? In short, does the *Journal*'s editorial page provide an adequate filter through which to interpret today's realities? Or could it be that the *Journal* is perpetuating illusions that are unrealistic in interpreting our global society and our role in it as Americans?

I'm OK—You're Radical

Beyond all the questions regarding the *Journal*'s editorial posture is the prior need to come to terms with our own attitudes—our frameworks—through which our essential values are shaped and reinforced. This has been the concern of transactional analysis (TA), an increasingly popular program among management today. (See *Business Week,* January 12, 1974.)* Through the process of transactional analysis, we find ourselves learning to understand even our enemies as we understand our different ego states—parental, adult, and child attitudes in solving our conflicts. This is not the place to expand upon transactional analysis, but the insights gained in our interpersonal relations can also be transferred to the issues confronting our global society.

Transactional analysis and other similar means are tools in enabling us to discover each other's humanity beyond the stereotyped labels we tag on others politically, vocationally, and socially. In a way, it is what Haverford College president John R. Coleman discovered when he used his sabbatical to learn how "the other side" thought and lived, becoming successively a ditch digger in Atlanta, a dishwasher and a sandwich and salad man in Boston, and finally a garbage collector in Maryland. "Reflecting on his experience, Coleman remembers with deep satisfaction a remark made to him by a 22-year-old foreman named Ron: 'You're the first good helper I've had in a long time. Keep it up.'" (*Time*, June 25, 1973.)

Breaking down the barriers, discovering each other's world, is necessary if we are not to be dictated to by yesterday's myths which are no longer operable in today's marketplace. So often we are

---

*For a fuller understanding of transactional analysis, see Eric Berne, *Games People Play* (Grove Press, 1964) and Thomas Harris, *I'm OK—You're OK* (Harper & Row, 1967, 1968, 1969).

captives to a world of labels; we find ourselves defending positions—conservative, liberal, independent, etc.—rather than seeking remedies to *fit* the complex problems confronting us. We need a deeper awareness of the attitudes we bring to our problems. Are these attitudes adequate and appropriate?

How often do we find ourselves dividing our world into those who are "OK" and those who are "radical"? This is, of course, an overstatement to highlight that anyone whose position differs considerably from ours on vital issues—politically, economically, socially, religiously, etc.—is placed in a "radical box" vis-à-vis our position. Also, we tend to limit our socializing to the crowd that we consider to be "OK." That is to say, "our crowd" shares the same attitudes, outlooks, and values. Of course we are seeking those with whom we are comfortable, but let's acknowledge the fact that we are being exposed to only one side of society. We usually know this intellectually, but our gut feelings tend to disregard the narrowness as we burrow ourselves deeper into our respective ghettos and value systems.

The amount of tolerance permitted in any one ghetto is considerable. In fact, each ghetto has a spectrum of views from extremists to conciliatory moderates. As long as the individual does not transcend the boundaries of his ghetto and its values, the individual is regarded as "OK," even if eccentric at times.

To break out of the ghetto and its basic support system is to become "radical," and therefore no longer "OK" to one's former "friends." Once the threshold of tolerance has been crossed, the individual is regarded disloyal. This is the greatest sin one can commit in organizational life today. Overstepping the ghetto-line is seen as a threat to all who remain behind, and the adventurer is called a "radical."

Our global island is divided between "OK's" and "radicals." Confrontations between these two groups are the hot and cold wars which have dominated the history of our twentieth century. In practice, most of our conversations throughout life are confined to our respective ghettos, which support our identities, hostilities, suspicions, and anxieties against other groups. It is almost as if those who "hate together stay together." Anyone seeking to build permanent bridges between groups is regarded with suspicion, and his credentials are questioned. Only the person who is sufficiently identified with a group and whose actions can be interpreted strictly in pragmatic terms of group-interest will be permitted to have any dealings with "the enemy." The diplomatic achievements with mainland China, the Soviet Union, and the Middle East are examples of this kind of contact.

Most of the prescriptions for the global island are uttered or written from the limited perspective of one ghetto or another. This is essentially a parochial outlook which does not reveal the total landscape of reality. In my own travels and residence in the United States and abroad, I have observed the uncanny domination of a ghetto mentality over a group. Actually this ghetto mentality is trans–national in character and consists of individuals sharing a common economic base or philosophy regardless of where they are living—Germany, Italy, Kenya, the Fiji Islands, or in the United States. The ethos is quite similar to the membership of a multi-national service organization like Rotary International.

The crucial task is to climb out of our respective ghettos and to discover the humanity on the other side. We must see, if only briefly as did Mr. Coleman, the complex problems which citizens of our global island face from their perspective as well as from ours. It's easy to think that we have already attained this understanding, but the subtleties and pressures for dialoguing in a monologue fashion continue to persist within every group.

Since the *Journal* is such an outstanding newspaper, enjoying not only a national but an international readership, it would be my hope that it would transcend its own parochialism. It needs to live up to its own golden rule—avoid illusions, be realistic. The *Journal,* I'm sure, does not consider itself parochial and might consider this observation to be unfair and inaccurate. Yet the thoughtful, well–written editorials in the *Journal* depict a style of dialoguing in a monologue fashion with many of the social and economic concerns of our world.

The *Journal*'s desire to uphold an "OK myth" to its readership might be comforting, but does it square with the realities? The editorial page might even receive high praise from some for upholding a value system that is no longer applicable to the human scene today. However, workable solutions to the complicated problems within the global village demand that we stop dialoguing in a monologue fashion, prescribed by a prior value system that conditions and selects the data which supports its particular philosophy.

There are other ghettos on the global island whose viewpoints need to be presented: the ghetto of the third world, the developing countries, and even the conclaves of our "enemies." In our nuclear era, we can't afford to avoid any viewpoint which affects the total welfare of the inhabitants on the global island. Not to reflect and be influenced by the total reality of the human scene within the interpretative editorial pages of the *Journal* is to do a disservice to the readership. If the *Journal* is truly to be "the Bible of Business" the whole story has to be told; the readership may not appreciate having its sacred myths or its sins exposed, but how else can we openly deal with reality? It may mean taking another look at our commitment to individualism, private vs. governmental investment, profit goals, the benefits of foreign acquisitions, and the entire idea of progress and productivity. The greatest tragedy for a business-oriented world community is to continue to buy myths that no longer fit realistically in the changing marketplace.

Let me illustrate our discussion at this point from the editorial page on October 3, 1972. On this day there appeared an article by P. T. Bauer, Professor of Economics at the London School of Economics, "The Case Against Foreign Aid," and also an editorial, "Rich Nations, Poor Nations," which basically endorsed Bauer's article. Bauer argues that providing government-to-government grants or soft loans to developing countries is not necessary and may be outright harmful to real economic progress. He illustrates his point by contending that small areas like Malaya, Ghana, and Hong Kong have progressed beautifully through private corporate capital without governmental grants.

Bauer's conviction is that "it is unwarranted to assume that because aid represents an inflow of resources, it must promote development. In fact, aid is at least as likely to retard development as to promote it." Furthermore, he points out, "Aid certainly removes resources from the donors. But it does not follow that it promotes development. To make the rich poor, does not make the poor rich." He therefore feels that "many advocates of aid are well intentioned, but not well informed. But by and large the aid crusade is a gigantic confidence trick." Even though there is evidence that cheating does go on in aid programs, to refer to governmental aid as essentially a "gigantic confidence trick" may be overstating the case.

In fact, Professor Bauer continues with his overstatement in listing a long line of groups involved in conning the public

> in part by playing on feelings of guilt, which however unfounded are nevertheless widespread. I think this coalition includes international agencies and government departments anxious to increase their activities and power; professional humanitarians with similar ambitions; disillusioned, bored, power-and-money-hungry academics; the churches which face spiritual collapse and seek a role as welfare agencies; temperamental do-gooders, frustrated by events at home; politicians in search of publicity; exporters in search of easy markets, and governments embarrassed by commodity surpluses.

Professor Bauer also adds that "there are also many people who welcome any argument or policy which in some way or other weakens the position of Western society, which for various political and emotional reasons they have come to dislike." In spite of all these shortcomings, Professor Bauer sadly concludes that governmental aid will continue, and he therefore wishes to change the method and criteria of allocation drastically. The direction of his changes would favor countries whose governments are more interested in governing than planning, who desire more liberal economic systems which minimize coercion and favor material progress and the improvement of living standards in behalf of the consumer.

There are many plausible as well as debatable points in Bauer's article. The *Journal*'s editorial commented,

> There may indeed be situations in the Third World where government-sponsored development is inevitable and desirable. The irony of the present situation is, however, that nearly all truly advanced nations arrived at their present state of advancement not through centralized economic management but through the decentralized dynamics of individual and

corporate enterprise.

This may be the case with our own economic past, but is it true today?

The editorial goes on to state that Robert S. McNamara, president of the World Bank, claims that the "industrial and developing nations are falling behind in their efforts to relieve hunger, illiteracy, and the threat of unmanageable population pressures." McNamara is therefore asking that the financial commitments to developing nations be increased by an average of 11% a year over the next five years. The editorial response to McNamara's concern was the following: "But money is not the entire problem, as Professor Bauer suggests. Those increments will be far more effective, if they can uncover ways to unlock the human potential in underdeveloped lands." There is, of course, a sweet reasonableness in the editorial's conclusion, but does it square with reality? To what extent is the business community itself constantly preoccupied with raising capital in order to survive or expand its operations? Is there not a tendency for big business to seek governmental subsidy when its own survival is at stake? And how is human potential to be unlocked if Bauer's prescription for governmental aid is followed? He suggests that preference be given to governments interested more in improving the roads and extending external contacts than in opening Western-type universities or in creating heavy engineering works. In short, it seems that the editorial page needs to step out of its own ghetto à la Coleman—and discover the larger world of "OK" people struggling to make life meaningful in their corner of the human community.

Corrective Attitudes for Rich and Poor

Indeed, we do live in an interrelated world—a global sandlot. Every war, every tension between rich and poor nations, has global implications. The war on poverty and injustice is not limited to our country; meeting these threats creatively is a global responsibility in a shrinking world. It is our responsibility to ensure that the benefits and advancements of technology in tomorrow's world will bring peace rather than war. We are challenged to be responsible with the resources at hand.

From a global perspective, there exists a real threat of increased violence by the poor and non-white peoples against the rich and largely white. Not only has the disparity between rich and poor increased in our day, but the technology employed by the rich nations is widening the gap of opportunities between a world of technically oriented "haves" and non-technically oriented "have-nots." There is an irrefutable relationship, according to McNamara, between violence and economic backwardness.

Since 1958, 87 percent of the very poor nations, 69 percent of the poor nations, and 48 percent of the middle-income nations have been plagued by internal strife and violence. By contrast, among the twenty-seven rich nations, only one nation has suffered a major internal upheaval within its boundaries. However, among the thirty-eight very poor nations, thirty-two have been victims of significant conflicts. Nations in this group have had on the average of two major outbreaks of violence per country in the past decade. In other words, if our desire is to have a safer world in which to live, our shrinking planet cannot neglect the needs of its poorer citizens: if not out of altruistic motivations, then simply out of enlightened self-interest.

Efforts are currently being undertaken to reduce the number of economically backward nations, and yet every indication is that the economic gulf widens rather than decreases. Since 1970, over one-half of the total population of the world has lived in the southern half of the planet. According to Dr. Kenneth Thompson of the Rockefeller Foundation, these people command less than one-sixth of the world's total goods and services.

> By 1975, dependent children under 15 years of age in these underdeveloped countries will equal the entire population of the developed nations of the world. By the end of this century, at present rates of growth, the most that the 80 underdeveloped nations who are members of the World Bank can hope for is a per capita income of $170 a year. In this same period, the U.S., whose current level is $2700, will have risen to $4500. ("The Challenge of the Future," *Worldview,* January, 1968.)

Related to this growing disparity is the now familiar issue of ecology. Environmental control has an expensive price tag. Within the present gulf between "have" and "have-not" nations, only the "haves" will be able to afford the massive ecological responsibilities which confront us. Is it possible that Western living standards of consumption and pollution have extended and further weakened the underdeveloped nations? Affluent man, exploding out of Europe and North America into South America, the islands of the Pacific, Africa, and Asia, has mined the land, the waterways, and the reefs with little thought of waste and contamination and has become accustomed to a consumer's life piled high with material goods. However, he has not included the ultimate cost to our vulnerable biological environment, not only at home but among the underdeveloped nations. The poor nations with lesser financial and technical resources will find great difficulty in correcting the imbalance caused by this kind of exploitation. Do we not have a responsibility to provide the necessary aid to restore the environmental controls needed throughout our shrinking world?

The situation is grave; we cannot escape the sobering question of peace or war between the world's "haves" and "have-nots." Whether we stand within the circle of our own society or take a global view of the situation, the issue of goods cannot be overlooked by the realistic person. Barbara Ward, international author and lecturer, notes that our situation today is both very complex and quite tragic. In her book *The Rich Nations and The Poor Nations* (p. 36, Norton, 1962), she writes:

> One part of mankind has undergone the revolutions of modernization and has emerged on the other side to a pattern of great and increasing wealth. But most of the rest of mankind has yet to achieve any of the revolutions; they are caught off balance before the great movement of economic and social momentum can be launched. Their old traditional world is dying. The new radical world is not yet born. This being so, the gap between the rich and the poor has become inëvitably the most tragic and urgent problem of our day.

How is the global situation seen through the poor man's filter? Is he as overwhelmed as we are with the complexities of the issues involved? Is he aware of his relatively poorer position in the world? The poor man's income is less than $200 per capita vs. $2,700 in the richest countries. His literacy level is 40%, as compared to 96% in the developed countries. His number of doctors per 100,000 people is 27, as compared to 134 in the wealthier countries. His life expectancy is 51 years, while 70 years is expected in the healthier countries. His infant mortality rate per 1,000 live births is 105, as compared to 27 in the richer countries. In most vital categories mentioned, the gap is widening between the poor man and the rich man in today's global village.

This is exactly why communism has such a wide appeal as seen through the poor man's filter. Today, one-third of mankind lives under the political control of communism; the influence of Marxism as a philosophy of life is even wider. The message of equality has meaning to those struggling for survival. From a Marxist orientation, the principle is clearly stated that men and nations alike will be organized "each according to his needs rather than each according to his capacities." As Barbara Ward points out, this principle "not only eliminates all class differences; it tries to establish a fundamental norm of 'need' which applies to every human being and should, in theory, do away with all differences in reward and status based on performance or special talent." (pp. 66-67)

What appeal would this have to people in India? Some 500 million people live in India, as much as two-fifths of all poor people in the uncommitted world, more commonly called the "Third World." The Third World (though it would be truer to describe it as the "two-thirds world") is largely made up of non-white peoples—a world of overpopulation, poverty, illiteracy, and a heritage of domination since the days of Christopher Columbus. Seeing the global village through the eyes of the Third World explains in large measure why the gospel according to Marxism is having such an impact.

Marxism is also having its appeal to the poor man in the United States. Look at a picture of poverty in this nation. Si Kahn's book *How People Get Power* (p. 124, McGraw-Hill, 1970) states it well:

> If anyone else still has illusions about this country, it's not the poor. They know that this country will spend $20 billion to put a man on the moon, but will not spend $20 to put a man on his feet. They know it will spend more to keep weevils from eating the cotton than to keep rats from eating the fingers of a baby in Harlem. They know it will pay a U.S. Senator over

> $100,000 a year not to plant cotton, but will not pay $1 to the families on his plantation not to raise hookworms in the stomachs of their own children.

The poor are crying out: "I needed a home, and you gave me Food Stamps;...I needed a job, and you got me on the Welfare;...My family was sick, and you gave us your used clothes;...I needed my pride and dignity as a man, and you gave me surplus beans."

If this represents the voice of the poor in the United States, the voice of the poor overseas is at least many times louder and in greater need. Nixon's historic trip to China, seen by millions of us, has for some time been the focal point of interest for the poor around the world. They have noted the dramatic shift in the Chinese people's improvement—millions who have left behind their days of starvation under the red banner of Mao and communism. From a global perspective, nations like ourselves must find ways to alleviate poverty in the world at a price other than that demanded by communism.

It is to the rich man's interest to address himself creatively to the poor man's filter; failure to do so is to ask for increased strife and endless war. The poor man will no longer buy the rich man's "gospel of poverty." Walter Peterson, President of the University of Dubuque, describes well the style and rationale of the gospel of poverty as proclaimed at the beginning of our century:

> The rich man had his park, but the poor man could look at it and enjoy it without the expense of maintaining it. Although others lived in stately mansions, they had to pay very heavily for the privilege. While the rich man may have had a valuable picture gallery, the poor man could see in the sunrise and sunset a splendor that no artist could ever capture. While the poor man did not possess some of the conveniences and delights of the more favored, in return he was free from many embarrassments to which the wealthy were subject. By the very simplicity and uniformity of his life the poor man was mercifully delivered from the great variety of cares that continually plagued his wealthy brother. Surely the plain meal eaten with relish and appetite by a poor man was more delicious than the most luxurious banquet.

This kind of rationalizing no longer impresses the poor man—white, black or yellow; American, African, or Asian.

It is therefore in the rich man's interest to discover the poor man's filter. As the courageous Archbishop Dom Helder Camara of Brazil has indicated, "The rich need the experience of the poor more than the poor need the technology of the rich." Yet, this is no easy thing to accomplish; it is difficult for anyone to wear another man's shoes, especially for the affluent. The observation has been made that the possession of material goods tends to make people conservative. The fear of losing what one possesses prevents us from acting in situations where risk is involved. On the other hand, those who have little or nothing are often freer from these fears and are willing to take risks needed. This is the state of most poor people who are aroused and no longer accepting of their lot in life. The fact is that the global sandlot is filled with pockets of poverty ready to explode.

Living as we are in a global village, let us imagine for the moment that the world's three billion people are symbolized by a village of 1,000 persons. In this village of 1,000 persons, only 164 people can be said to be living a moderately satisfied life, while 836 exist under the most varying degrees of desperation imagined—poverty, disease, economic and political oppressions, conditions of degradation, etc. Our question: how do the 164 privileged communicate or relate with the 836 who are desperate? Remember, in this village of 1,000 persons there is instantaneous communication. The poor are acutely aware of their plight. They have seen their neighbor's refrigerators, washers, dryers, and automobiles, and wonder why they are without them. Centuries of acquiescence to the inevitability of poverty are at an end. *The gospel of poverty has given way to the gospel of Marxism.* Hostility and resentment at injustice are growing daily, determining the histories of many nations and persons. The pressures for reform, rebellion, and revolution are fermenting among the majority within our symbolized village. The issue of securing justice without violence is the paramount question of the hour within the village. It is precisely at this point that we need to widen our areas of mutual need.

Anyone, rich or poor, who is disillusioned about reality is a potential revolutionary. By the same token, everyone is also a conservative when protecting his vital interests—self-respect, family, property, etc. The task today is to discover and support the overlapping areas of self-interest and mutual need for rich and poor.

To fail to do so is to invite violence.

Violence has many dimensions. For the poor man, the death of a young woman in childbirth is violent; the slow starvation of the mind and body of a child is violent; hunger is violent; pain is violent; oppression is violent; early death is violent; illiteracy is violent; and the death of hope is the most violent of all. For the rich man, the loss of property is violent; the loss of status is violent; and the loss of savings is violent. In short, rich and poor are in a common arena of turbulence. The aim of each is to get home safe, with something meaningful to share with one's family.

How then can rich and poor help each other? Is a program of mutual self-interest possible? Is a coalition of rich and poor realistic? Many who have been involved in the struggle of either camp would ridicule the suggestion of creating such a coalition since the uplifted fist on either side is ready to battle rather than to negotiate. Is the inevitable outcome one of strife and bloodshed?

Archbishop Dom Helder Camara describes the situation by saying, "Which is more difficult and more exciting: to humanize subhuman men wretched by misery, or to humanize supermen dehumanized by luxury? The two tasks complement each other in such a way that the realization of each is dependent on that of the other." Thus the archbishop calls for a "revolution through peace" to defuse the M bomb, "the misery bomb" more terrible than the A bomb or the H bomb.

How can this be done, except through the discovery of each other's humanity? The following are suggestions for reaching the goal: First, by working for the mutual *concientizaciôn*—literally, "consciousness-raising"—of each other's true identity. No social change can take place without an enlightened awareness resulting in the breakdown of mutual stereotypes. Second, finding an effective program of involvement for the "middle-class" in developed countries willing to risk their corporate structures if necessary in order to be responsible and responsive to the demands of the poor. Third, experiments in creative "exchange" programs. New ventures and understanding may emerge from extensive observations and experiences of each other's life-style. Fourth, new projects must be directed toward economic growth and redistribution of wealth. Fifth, more equitable distribution of the benefits of reform programs that preserve human pride and personal identity. Programs that call for local participation in the decision-making process will enhance communication between rich and poor. In short, both groups must recognize that coexistence is the only viable option. Without this recognition, mutual destruction will eliminate any hope of achieving an abundant life on today's global sandlot.

God and the Country Club

The desire for an abundant life is a common goal throughout the global sandlot. The interpretations of that abundant life may differ, but a material basis for its existence is undeniable. We are all materialists—capitalist, Marxist, Christian, Jew, Muslim, etc. For instance, I am a Christian materialist; I take my material clues from those essential aspects of my faith—my belief in God the Creator and in the incarnation of Jesus Christ, the Word of God made flesh. (See my book *Grace, Guts and Goods: How to Stay Christian in an Affluent Society,* Thomas Nelson Inc., 1971.) My neighbor may base his materialism on some other grounds. How he wishes to save or consume his material possessions may be based on yet another set of standards. He may wish to join the country club or he may not; his rising expectations in life, however, demand that he be in a position to be able to choose.

This concern for the abundant life was made vividly clear to me one day in a conversation with an owner of a large meat store. He was an ambitious proprietor in his forties who was proud of his new establishment. I asked him, "What do you want in life?" "Making a good living for my wife and children," he replied instantly. He went on to say that he had largely accomplished that goal and was still restless. "In fact," he said, "I thought that after I had my new store and bought our new home near the country club, that I had it made. . . but my troubles only began. When my customers learned of my expensive new home, some wished me well, others were silent, and twenty-five of my customers left me in disgust! They felt I was making an unfair profit at their expense. Why did they have to leave me? Can't they understand, all I want is a good life for my family!"

I asked him, "What do you want to be remembered for after your death?" He replied, "That's a strange question. I was thinking about that myself the other day. How will people remember me?...that I was a good provider, husband, father? Of course, my family and relatives will think of me in these terms. But what will my customers and business associates think?...that I was a decent man who charged a fair price, paid my bills on time, that I was a good butcher who sold the highest quality of meat? To tell the truth, the question depresses me. It makes me wonder if my time and energies are being well spent. Is the good life what we think it is?" he asked.

A friend told me once, "The good life is to be able to go first-class in everything." Occasionally, I have lunch or dinner at the country club. The food is rather good, the atmosphere is certainly first-class, but is it the good life? Don't misunderstand me; I'm not condemning it. I simply want us to focus on our priorities—our understandings of the good life. What follows in our discussion will be seen from our perspective of the good life.

To reach the good life, our business culture has long advocated "honesty is the best policy," plus hard work, discipline, fear of God, and a healthy family life. This outlook still holds for many, but for others the individualistic virtues of initiative and competition, the efficient allocation of resources through the market, consumer needs, etc., have become too awesome and too complicated today. The distance seems to widen between them and the pot of gold at the end of the rainbow. According to Dun & Bradstreet, Inc., the number of business failures on record in one recent year (1972) was 9,566, amounting to a loss of over $2 billion.

It is reported elsewhere that one million Americans have gone bankrupt since 1967, and the total consumer debt at the end of 1972 stood at a staggering $158 billion. (Richard J. Pietschmann, "Personal Bankruptcy: The Jekyll and Hyde of Going Broke," *Mainliner,* May, 1974.) Even if one didn't go into business for himself, there is no sure-fire way of staying out of poverty today. *U.S. News and World Report* (May 28, 1973) informs us that there are 21 million Americans, counting dependents, who work for a living yet remain in poverty. This embraces one of every ten Americans.

It might help our spirits to mention here the historic White House Conference (February 7-9, 1972) on the "Industrial World

Ahead," which announced in its summary findings *(A Look at Business in 1990,* U.S. Government Printing Office, Washington, D.C., November, 1972), what we can expect to have in 1990:

(1) A gross national product of almost 2½ trillion dollars.
(2) A 36-hour work week.
(3) Sixty percent of all families with income over $15,000.
(4) Six out of seven families owning their own homes.

Yet, in the *here and now*, such predictions sound apocalyptic to millions. Today's inflation even makes it difficult for some to stay honest. The *Journal* captured the mood in one of its feature stories with the headline, **"Let's Make a Deal—Many Shoppers Find Some Real Bargains—By Switching Tags"** (July 30, 1973). One store manager viewed tag switchers as not the normal run of shoplifters; they're amateurs who normally never dream of stealing. Today we accept, if not altogether approve, the fact that there are various degrees of dishonesty, somewhat akin to the old tradition of "white lies" and "black lies." Another *Journal* story, under the banner, **"Looking for Work—As Economy Tightens, Far More Applicants Seek Unskilled Jobs,"** (June 5, 1974). This news story reported how 40 city meter-reader openings drew 2,800 people in Los Angeles. In addition, there are countless numbers of college graduates now joining the lincs of unskilled employment. All this might not seem so bad if we could view the situation as a temporary moment in time, unless of course, you are one of the unhappy victims. It appears that we are increasingly thwarted, going nowhere, certainly not to the country club!

All of the foregoing illustrates that "making it" the American way cannot be taken for granted nor can it be guaranteed by any fixed formula. Life is hard and also a challenge, with much luck along the way. The businessman who has failed and then finally succeeds knows this. His past experiences may serve to harden him or may spur him on to a spirit of thankfulness and generosity.

Those who are hardened will see profit-taking as a way of life. John Ruskin expressed it candidly when he wrote, "The art of making yourself rich in the ordinary mercantile economic sense, is therefore equally and necessarily the art of keeping your neighbor poor." (Quoted in Karl Menninger, *Whatever Became of Sin?* p. 150,

Hawthorn Books, Inc., 1973.) This has been called "cowboy capitalism," the reckless pursuit of profits at all costs. The apparent motto at the Harvard Business School, after examining hundreds of case studies, is the distilled common sense conclusion *"that the maximization of long-range profit is why God hath created the earth."* This in turn is interpreted to be "the American way, that outworn, hilariously twisted and disfigured ethic which urges people to compete for the sake of competing, achieve for the sake of achieving, win for the sake of winning, and which honors him who does all this without pause or letup—the fastest, the richest, the smartest, the nicest, the sportiest, the artiest; because things wouldn't be the way they are unless God meant them to be." (Peter Cohen, *The Gospel According to the Harvard Business School,* p. 328, Doubleday & Co., 1973.) This profit-oriented, pragmatic professional hasn't had time for anyone, not even for himself or his country club.

As a result of such hard-nosed profit-orientation, the public image of "The Ugly Businessman," (January 23, 1974) emerges. The *Journal* editorial warns the businessman not to forsake his basic mission in spite of his present unpopularity with the public. The businessman's task is to bring about economic stability, not to worry about his fallen image or buy into social panaceas that undercut basic economic fundamentals. The editorial concludes that "the Ugly Businessman can't become one of the beautiful people simply by climbing on the bandwagon of dreamers."

On the other hand, business leaders concerned about their roles and social responsibilities can't take comfort in such an editorial. They are raising questions concerning the validity of those "basic economic fundamentals" which govern our business culture. President John Adams, Jr. of the Hanover Insurance Companies comments,

> If in fact the primary or overriding purpose of business is to make a profit, then the free enterprise system should and will be self-destructive. The idea that profit per se is good no longer stands examination. Profit is good if the process of making a profit results in satisfying the need of the consumer more effectively and more efficiently than a nonprofit system.

Mr. Adams sounds quite different from the businessman who is solely profit motivated. Realistically, he observes "that consumerism is here to stay, that business is the cause of consumerism, and that consumerism will destroy business unless businessmen realize that satisfaction of the consumer and not profit is the purpose of business."

President Adams is not alone in his observations. Peter Drucker, management specialist, defines profits "not as a company's purpose but as an objective requirement of economic activity. Profit is seen as a minimum need of the corporation—not as a maximum 'goal' of business." For Drucker, "'businessmen who talk about profit maximization are doing more to hurt the system than anything else. They are merely convincing people that there is no defense of the system.'" ("Peter Drucker: A new compendium for management," *Business Week,* February 9, 1974. See also his latest book, *Management: Tasks•Responsibilities•Practices•* Harper & Row, 1973, 1974.) While earning a "fair profit" is important, it is not the heart of the matter within the larger societal context in which business finds its own nourishment.

What is more important than profits is satisfying the consumer needs, enhancing his quality of life. The businessman who responds to his neighbors in a spirit of thankfulness and generosity is not only acknowledging his Creator but is following a program of long-range pragmatism which will also benefit his own business. Such an outlook provides the business community with a new badge of legitimacy. Irwin Miller, Chairman of Cummins Engine, says, "The corporation is not unlike the individual. It achieves a good reputation if it deserves it. Image and reputation follow performance and service to the community." (Max Ways, "Business Needs to Do a Better Job of Explaining Itself," *Fortune,* September, 1972.)* When business maintains a social audit of its activities, its profits and its presence will receive wider social acceptance.

---

*See also in this connection Neil H. Jacoby, *Corporate Power and Social Responsibility* (Macmillan, 1973); Meinolf Dierkes and Raymond A. Bauer, ed., *Corporate Social Accounting* (Praeger Publisher, 1973) and Charles W. Powers, ed., *People/Profits: The Ethics of Investment,* (Council on Religion and International Affairs, 1972).

Beyond corporate social responsibility and resulting from it will be a more meaningful role for the corporate executive. He will be promoted from being an employee of the stockholders, hired to maximize their profits, and will be seen as an arbiter among competing interests for the common welfare. Young people who are shying away from business careers today might be more attracted to this enhanced role. (Henry C. Wallich, "How Business Can Rescue Capitalism," *Fortune,* March, 1972.) Will business be able to shift then from a strict profit orientation to a self-interest policy of generosity in helping to contribute to a more socially acceptable environment? Will the business community come to see that *generosity is the best policy* in our imperfect world?

Before we conclude this chapter's discussion, we must consider one of the basic questions underlying any effective program of generosity. This is the issue concerning the distribution of wealth. Can enlightened self-interest administer a program of generosity without social legislation? In an editorial entitled "Probing Human Behavior" (May 29, 1973), the *Journal* frankly states that we just don't know "What makes man tick?" The conviction of the editorial is that we cannot fit our social ills, nor all human beings and their behavior, into narrow categories. Therefore, since we know so little about individual motivation and reaction, the editorial warns "editorial writers as well as sociologists, who act as though we alone have the answers for improving or regulating human behavior through social legislation" to pause and reconsider their positions. While I can appreciate the sincere humility of the editorial stance, it will not satisfy the relentless pursuit of equality by millions in America and countless others throughout the global village.

This hunger for equality, more than any other single value, is undoubtedly the mainspring of radicalism. "What one's attitude is toward equality in the whole complex of social, cultural, and economic goods tells us almost perfectly whether one is radical, liberal, or conservative." (Robert Nisbet, "The Pursuit of Equality," *The Public Interest,* Spring, 1974.) This is indeed a delicate and touchy subject for many. It is certainly a delicate subject to the approximately 150 companies found most often in *Fortune*'s 500 list, whose controlling ownership rests either in the hands of a single individual or among the members of a single family. (Ralph L. Andreano, ed., *Superconcentration/Supercorporation: A Collage of Opinion on the Concentration of Economic Power,* Warner Modular Publications, Inc., 1973.) It has been estimated that 4.4% of our population owns most of the wealth in America. To this select core of economic elite, the subject of equality may produce all kinds of fears and anxieties. Surprisingly, for the remaining 95.6% of the population, the economic elite continue to symbolize a distant goal of opportunity. How long will the bulk of the population (especially the middle-class) continue to be inspired before they become completely disillusioned with the American way? This is one of the unknown questions of the future.

For the present time, Americans have placed their trust upon the equality of opportunity as the means of reaching their country-club goals. In John Rawls' study, *A Theory of Justice* (pp. 73-75, The Belknap Press of Harvard University Press, Cambridge, 1971), the author argues that equality of opportunity exists only if there is the same probability for successful results. It is his contention that inequalities of birth and natural endowment are undeserved; therefore these individuals must in some way be compensated for their disadvantages if we are truly to treat all people as equal and consider the opportunities before them as real possibilities. Only in this way can we really have equality of opportunity and enhance the quality of life for the total citizenry. Professor Rawls' position is what Harvard sociologist Daniel Bell calls a "principle of redress." (See his book *The Coming of Post-Industrial Society,* Basic Books, Inc., 1973). Professor Rawls considers the establishment of a realistic and just basis for equality to be the central problem in our society today.

Related to the issue of equality and wealth distribution are proposals such as tax grants for the poor, reform of the welfare structures, an extension of social security benefits, and the implications arising if an economic policy of scarcity is followed. (See John Kenneth Galbraith, *Economics and the Public Purpose,* Houghton Mifflin, 1973.) Herbert Stein, former Chairman of the President's Council of Economic Advisors, wrote a critical appraisal of Galbraith's book in the *Journal* (October 16, 1973). He indicated that the author's advocacy of a simpler life, low consumption, much leisure, and much contemplation will have serious negative effects upon the labor force and consumer needs. Mr. Galbraith's "inefficient, unproductive society," claims Mr. Stein, "does not equally offer its members the choice of living the life of affluence if they prefer that." Perhaps Tallulah Bankhead summed up Mr. Stein's desire when she said, "I've been poor and I've been rich and, believe me, rich is better."

We need to be reminded of another view: "As more and more Americans reach advanced levels of affluence, the role of money in their lives will inevitably diminish and may in fact become perverse. We have no illusion that man lives by electric toasters alone." (Peter Passell and Leonard Ross, *The Retreat from Riches: Affluence and Its Enemies,* p. 185, The Viking Press, 1971.) Paul A. Samuelson writes in the Foreword to this book that

> without doubt, the burning question of the day, especially among young people, has to do with our national growth. "To William James, the bitch goddess of America was success. Isn't worship of a zooming GNP a reversion to idolatry of the golden calf?" As one earnest student put it, "To me, GNP is gross national pollution. I wish it could halve, not double."

Where do you stand in this current debate? How much materialism is necessary for the good life? Should limits be placed on our material prosperity, realizing the limited supply of resources available on our global sandlot? Is it possible that God will take our country clubs from us?

Our final chapter will discuss a more encompassing gospel than what the *Journal* offers. The need today is for a more enriched diet of realistic hopes and purposes that will point us, individually and collectively, beyond our bicentennial anniversary to a vital and meaningful life-style in a world without boundaries.

VI

Hope in a Watergate World

Do we find ourselves grasping for hope amidst the contradictions, confusion, and realities of our Watergate world? Is the "Watergate world" limited to specific events, or isn't it more accurately a description of our human existence? To read the many articles and editorials in the *Journal* on Watergate is to see the human spirit oscillating between hope and near-hopelessness. We would like to share ex-Senator Harold Hughes' conviction that "God can and will use Watergate as a rebirth of this nation." Only with the passing of time will we ever know for sure if this has been accomplished.

In the meantime, we can concur with the respected Vermont Royster of the *Journal* (October 17, 1973) that the public morality is in a sad state of affairs; we need to insist upon some absolute standards for our public officials. Awareness of our plight does promise some measure of hope. Of course, we need to be ever watchful that our hopes are never frozen nor married to past models that no longer prove adequate. Whatever the case, it is evident that hope belongs to the human situation; to hope is to be human.

Without vision or hope, our prospects as a nation for continued greatness are diminished. The crises of recent years demand honest recognition of our depletion of values. We have been living in a state of hypocrisy vis-à-vis our cherished myths. The times now require that we overhaul our American myths and dreams—update them along lines of realistic hope. Such hope calls for a *revolutionary rebirth* with the tenacity, foresight, and courage of our forefathers.

Robert L. Bartley, the *Journal*'s editor of the editorial page, has written ("Irving Kristol and Friends," May 3, 1972) that "a society, culture or civilization is ultimately held together not by its formal institutions but by informal things—traditions, values, feelings and expectations shared by its citizens and imposing on them certain disciplines." If such is the case, then we need to pay closer attention to the informal fibers that shape a society. Are we willing to identify which informal fibers are absolutely essential to our institutional life? In short, is it possible for us to be committed to a community of values embracing past traditions and yet attentive to tomorrow's world?

The Search for a Community of Values

Values are the goals, the ends, and the ultimate concerns supported individually and collectively by society. Behind these values are beliefs and attitudes not always articulated. One hundred years ago the present value crisis would have been described as a spiritual crisis. The ultimate grounding of a value system has usually been sought in some metaphysical or religious assumption.* Part of our current malaise is that we have rejected or ignored this metaphysical or theological base vital to a value system. Theologian Hugh T. Kerr of Princeton in an issue of *Theology Today* (April, 1974), has put forth the following thesis:

> *When the religious value system that once supported the culture is ignored or rejected, the moral and ethical value system plunges into chaos.* When "moral values" are no longer sustained by "religious values," they apparently aren't sustained by anything else.

The above assertion is given further credence by Kerr with quotes from Malcolm Muggeridge, Joseph Campbell, and Erich Fromm. According to Muggeridge (from the transcript of the *Firing Line* program, "Has America Had It?" September 16, 1973), the

---

*Books helpful in understanding the nature of values are the following: Charles Fried, *An Anatomy of Values* (Harvard University Press, 1970); Lon L. Fuller, *The Morality of Law* (Yale University Press, 1969); Reinhold Niebuhr, *Moral Man and Immoral Society* (Charles Scribner's Sons, 1932); Milton Rokeach, *Beliefs, Attitudes and Values: A Theory of Organization and Change* (Jossey-Boss Inc., 1969); James Sellers, *Public Ethics: American Morals and Manners* (Harper & Row, 1970); Francis X. Sutton, Seymour E. Harris, Carl Kaysen, James Tobin, *The American Business Creed* (Harvard University Press, 1956); Max Weber, *The Protestant Ethic and the Spirit of Capitalism* (Charles Scribner's Sons, 1958); Walter A. Weisskopf, *Alienation and Economics* (Delta, 1971).

well-known British author and journalist and former self-proclaimed agnostic:

> Basically what is happening, I think, in the world is [the dominance of] scientific materialism's view of life (that we can by means of science solve all our problems, create for ourselves a happy, fulfilled life by our own efforts), [and] that the Christian religion on which after all our civilization was founded no longer has any real validity. . . . First of all, we'll abolish all sense of a moral order, which is very largely done now, and having abolished all sense of a moral order, it seems to me almost inevitable that every other form of order will likewise disintegrate. . . . In my opinion, we are witnessing the total moral breakdown of a way of life. . . . Chesterton . . . said, "When people don't believe in God, they don't then believe in nothing, they believe in anything."

A second quotation is from Campbell's recent book, *Myths to Live By* (Viking Press, pp. 10f, 1972):

> Literally read, [religious] symbolic forms have always been—and still are, in fact—the support of their civilizations, the supports of their moral orders, their cohesion, vitality, and creative powers. With the loss of them, there follows uncertainty, and with uncertainty, disequilibrium, since life . . . requires life-supporting illusions; and where these have been dispelled, there is nothing secure to hold on to, no moral law, nothing firm. . . . There is everywhere in the civilized world a rapidly rising incidence of vice and crime, mental disorders, suicides and dope-addictions, shattered homes, impudent children, violence, murder, and despair. These are facts: I am not inventing them.

This third quotation results from an interview by Alden Whitman with Fromm *(The New York Times,* p. 33, December 15, 1973), the prolific author and psychologist, who escaped Hitler's Germany about forty years ago. He views America, which once gave so much hope to him, as presently obsessed by a passion for destruction:

> "There is still a moral residue in America composed of our religious and humane tradition in which the proper goal of society is to serve its members. . . .
>
> What is urgent now if we are not to continue on the path of destructiveness and national suicide is a renewal of *a sense of general religious values."* (Italics added.)

To the above quotations, let me add another from Paul Freund, a moral and legal philosopher of worldwide eminence, a professor at the Harvard Law School, who participated in The Rockefeller Foundation Conference on "Values in Contemporary Society" (July 13, 1972) from which this quote is taken:

> It seems to me that whatever you call them—values, virtues, or fundamentals—there is a considerable thirst among ordinary people, students and ordinary people, for moorings. Having lost, by and large, their religious moorings, they are looking for something to put in its place, and I think there is an opportunity here. People are isolated. They feel impotent. But that is not the end of the story. They are aware—a great many people are aware—and they are looking for some way of understanding, meaning or purpose, of making themselves felt, of making themselves count.

Today's Watergate world (and there are many "Watergates") has intensified our search for a community of values. One clear indication of the present morass is that we no longer have any heroes—American leaders to whom we can point with pride. With the loss of our heroes, we have lost our morale. The question is whether there is any visible value system that we can still cling to other than an old-fashioned piety that no longer appears to motivate us within the complexities of our present society. Is it possible for us to design a value system that we can call American and share on a global basis? And can we have a visible value system without the dimension of transcendence? Can a value system be any more than a "cut-flower ethic" without religious and metaphysical roots? Paul Tillich has reminded us, "Religion is the substance of culture, culture is the form of religion."

Given the fact of our global awareness, no promises can be made that a universal community of values can be established. Nevertheless, the issues of values needs to be raised if there is to be any rescue from the present confusion of our value-free stance towards many new problems facing us. Without a strategy based upon value priorities, we will not know where to begin or how much of our energy and resources should be expended. Efforts toward value frameworks will go far in giving direction to our policies in both the public and private sectors of life.

Dr. Ralph Siu, Chairman of the Academy for Contemporary Problems in Columbus, Ohio, has aptly described the current as a shift from the game of American to Chinese baseball. Chinese baseball is played much like American baseball—the same field, players, bat, ball, and method of keeping score. The batter stands at home plate, and as the pitcher zips the ball down the alley, the one and only one difference occurs. The difference, which is unique to Chinese baseball, allows that once the ball leaves the pitcher's hand and as long as the ball is in the air, *anyone can move any of the bases anywhere.*

Chinese baseball, unlike American baseball, illustrates that everything is changing all the time, not only the events themselves but also the very rules governing the events and the criteria of values. *There are no fixed points of reference.* It is therefore essential for the players to keep their eye not only on the fast moving ball as it leaves the pitcher's hand but also on the fast shifting bases as well. We are faced today with Chinese baseball, but nostalgically long to continue with American baseball rooted in familiar but outmoded platitudes.

To meet the pressures of the present, Dr. Siu indicates that we must cultivate the *instantaneous apprehension of the totality of the human situation* at any given moment. As we grasp the instantaneous apprehension of the totality, we will be in a better position to find a particular thread that will unite the crazy quilt of existence confronting us. In order to test out the threads that we pick, we must practice *the art of subsuming and resonating.* According to Dr. Siu, the art of subsuming and resonating will indicate whether our thread of interpretation for that situation subsumes all the particular factors involved and resonates with each of them meaningfully. If our thread meets this test, we have then established a value base for that situation. As we analyze various situations, discovering other threads of interpretation, we will be better able to construct a meaningful and unified value system.

The laboratory for experimenting with varied value systems could be our schools and communities through courses and town meetings. The running theme might be "The Art of Living" (Siu's suggestion) or "Survival of the Species—sos" (labor leader and author Gus Tyler's suggestion).* Such seminars would aim to clarify value considerations within our society. In addition to seminars, it is hoped that a wider range of citizens than academic professionals will see the importance of sabbatical programs for reflection and researching of attitudes, beliefs, values, and practices encountered during the normal routine of responsibilities.**

The objective and the premise for such experiences will be the certification at the grass roots of those values necessary to make human life more human, acknowledging the unique and intrinsic worth of each individual. From such dialogues and cooperative involvement the emergence of a community of values might become a reality.

Since we are a society of unique individuals, we will favor a countless variety of values. This variety has become exceedingly more complicated since technology has made us into a global village. Dr. Denis Goulet, a research fellow at the Center for the Study of Development of Social Change at Cambridge, Massachusetts, indicates (see his article in *The Christian Century,* April 24, 1974, "The World of Underdevelopment: A Crisis in Values") at least four basic characteristics of modern life. They are the following:

- The enormous scale of all basic operations;
- The technological complexity of production and organization;
- The multiple inter-dependencies linking all units of societies, whether they be local, regional, national or international;
- The ever-shortening time lag between stimuli and the required response.

In addition to these characteristics of modern life, there is also the

---

*Mr. Tyler's provocative article is found in *Change* (May-June, 1970) entitled "Everybody's Core Curriculum." Mr. Tyler is assistant president of the International Ladies' Garment Workers' Union.

**See for an expansion of this theme Kenneth Lamott, "Proposed: That Every American Should Get One Year Off in Every Seven," *Esquire,* February, 1974; Jon M. Healy, "The Sabbatical-Executive Style," *Dun's,* March, 1974; and Eli Goldston, "Executive Sabbaticals: About to take off?" *Harvard Business Review,* Sept.-Oct., 1973.

"alienation in abundance" which is no less dehumanizing than the "alienation in misery." A minority in the global village are primarily interested in maximizing their happiness and self-fulfillment, while the majority are concerned with minimizing their suffering. In today's global village neither side can live in isolation from the other; the reality is that they are organically linked together. This will have wide implications in itemizing any list of values.

In any final reckoning of values, each of us must come to terms with our preferences. How do individuals determine what has value for them? We must identify our ultimate concerns—what we are willing to protect at all costs. These can be described as having personal value for us. An initial list of such values might include human relationships, self-concept, possession, vocation, causes, etc. Whatever we are willing to defend, to pay for personally, has value then for us. It may be described as our religion—our ultimate concern or end in life.

In a pluralistic democracy such as ours, there will obviously exist numerous goals and ends which need to be honored and respected. Can any consensus be found in the context of this plurality? In raising this question we need to admit not only that countless values exist within society, but even more so that *we need to value the valuing process itself within a democracy.* It should never be taken for granted. The valuing process itself should serve along with the metaphysical and religious presuppositions as the essential base for a value system. The search for values in contemporary society must give equal consideration to its content and to its process.

To affirm the value of the democratic process implies adequate grassroots expression, but also an affirmation of the intrinsic worth of individuals—their integrity—the fact that persons are ends and not means, the need of freedom and the importance of tolerance. Also implied are the benefits of inefficiency and the necessity for conflict and even disorder at times, if we are to be more than a totalitarian society which is monolithic and obsessed with rational efficiency, social order, and uniformity. Ideally, the American goal has been the emergence of a "co-willing" community. It is out of this "co-willing" context that a "community" of the many is achieved. "This 'community' of the many is not a mere addition of wills, rather, it is a new kind of will, a communal will" (Herbert Richardson, "Values and Priorities in Planning for America," *The Church Woman,* January 1974). For Americans then, the valuing process is as important as any listing of values themselves.

Having underlined the vital importance of the valuing process, the selection of values themselves could follow a threefold development as indicated by the authors of *Values and Teaching* (Louis Raths, Merrill Harmin, and Sidney Simon, p. 30, Charles E. Merrill Publishing Co., 1966). Their description can be summarized in this way:

CHOOSING: (1) freely
(2) from alternatives
(3) after thoughtful consideration of the consequences of each alternative
PRIZING: (4) cherishing, being happy with the choice
(5) willing to affirm the choice publicly
ACTING: (6) doing something with the choice
(7) repeatedly, in some pattern of life.

Through a process of consciously choosing, prizing, and acting, we can arrive at some listing of our values, as we bear in mind that we are living in the context of Chinese baseball. Underscoring the fact that the human situation is dynamic, we will need to equip our interior beings with sufficient "psychic space" so as not to rush the process or to make ourselves think that we can achieve a definitive list of values for all time. As we are engaged in the common pursuit of clarifying our values, our sense of community will be in a stage of becoming and should provide sufficient motivation to overcome feelings of disappointment, frustration, and the nostalgic longing for fixed points of reference. Values are actually the ultimate base for which a society finds its raison d'etre. Values justify the kind of society we wish to have. Can we aim for anything less than a diligent search for a community of values?

Value Conflicts

Inevitably our search will be faced with conflicting value claims. What kind of trade-offs will we make? What are the guidelines and priorities that will determine our game plan? Ian H. Wilson of General Electric, in an address on "Education and the Values Revolution," has highlighted some of the areas of shifting value concerns:

> From an emphasis on quantity ('more'), toward considerations of quality ('better');
> From the concept of independence, toward the concept of interdependence (of nations, institutions, individuals, all natural species);
> From mastery over nature, toward living in harmony with it;
> From competition, toward cooperation;
> From doing and planning, toward being;
> From the primacy of technical efficiency, toward considerations of social justice and equity;
> From the dictates of organizational convenience, toward the aspirations of self-development in an organization's members;
> From authoritarianism and dogmatism, toward participation;
> From uniformity and centralization, toward diversity and pluralism;
> From the concept of work as hard, unavoidable and a duty, toward work as purpose and self-fulfillment and a recognition of leisure as a valid activity in its own right.

Behind these shifting value concerns are changing attitudes basic to our prevailing business culture. The attitudes comprise for many the American way of life. Such basic beliefs must be critically re-examined in the light of new requirements and needs as we shape our destiny for the next two hundred years. First, we need to question the high priority on winning "at any cost" within our society. As we recover the transcendent dimension necessary to a viable value system, we will rediscover that success and "winning at any cost is a losing proposition because life is not something to be won; it is a gift from God" (James M. Wall, "The Value System Of A Faithless People," *The Christian Century,* May 29, 1974). This drive for success in our business culture has been one of the reasons for the tensions and inconsistencies felt throughout our development of markets and our neglect of morals during rapid economic growth.

Second, our belief in individualism, and related concerns for equality and opportunity, represented society as no more than the sum of the individuals in it. This attitude should be updated. Society has its own "special and urgent needs, and the survival and the self-respect of the individuals in it depend on the recognition of those needs. There are few who can get their kicks â la John Wayne, although many try. Individual fulfillment for most depends on a place in a community, an identity with a whole, a participation in an organic social process" (George Cabot Lodge, "Business and the changing society," *Harvard Business Review,* March-April 1974). The fact is that individualism in America, with few exceptions, has already evolved into "interest group pluralism."

Third, our belief in individual rights directly supported the sanctity of property rights. According to Lodge,

> Today there is a new right which clearly supersedes property rights in political and social importance. It is the right to survive—to enjoy income, health, and other rights associated with membership in the American community or in some component of that community, including a corporation.

Property rights are increasingly being subordinated to essential human rights for all persons in tomorrow's emerging community.

Fourth, our belief and prevailing attitude that competition is American is seriously questioned by big business today as it seeks to satisfy consumer desires. Listen to the representatives of free enterprise: "Don't visit that old idea of competition on us. The public interest requires ITT to be big and strong at home so that it can withstand the blows of Allende in Chile, Castro in Cuba, and the Japanese in general. Before you apply the antitrust laws to us, the Secretary of the Treasury, the Secretary of Commerce, and the Council of Economic Advisors should meet to decide what, in the light of our balance-of-payments problems and domestic economic difficulties, the national interest is." (Used by Lodge and taken from the *Hearings Before the Committee on the Judiciary, United States Senate, 92nd Congress, Second Session on Nomination of Richard G. Kleindienst of Arizona to Be Attorney General,* Washington: Government Printing office, 1972). It should be noted again these are the advocates of free enterprise who are arguing against competition in an open market.

Fifth, the belief in a limited state nurtured the general attitude that "the least government is the best government." Today, government is playing an expanding role forced by the complexity of our situation. It is becoming increasingly, in Lodge's words,

> the setter of our sights and the arbiter of community needs. Inevitably, it will take on unprecedented tasks of coordination, priority setting, and planning in the largest sense. It will need to become far more efficient and authoritative, capable of making the difficult and subtle trade-offs which now confront us—for example, between environmental purity and energy supply.

Any nostalgic longing for a limited state must be questioned as naïve if we are to plan realistically for the future. The important issue now is how democratically inclusive is the input into the decision-making process.

Sixth, our belief in specialization as the clue to material growth and progress is seriously being challenged today. The emphasis that if we attend to the parts, as experts and specialists, the whole will take care of itself is not the case. The old idea of scientific specialization has given way today to a new consciousness of the interrelatedness of all things. As Lodge says:

> Spaceship earth, the limits of growth, the fragility of our life-supporting biosphere have dramatized the ecological and philosophical truth that everything is related to everything else. Harmony between the works of man and the demands of nature is no longer the romantic plea of conservationists. It is an absolute rule of survival, and thus it is of profound ideological significance, subverting in many ways all of the Lockean ideas.

The demand for integration and interdisciplinary approaches to the issues before us will be the normal style of operation for tomorrow.

Seventh, our belief that if we only produce enough goods the needs of our global society will be met is seriously questioned today. Nature's resources are limited; to look upon the production of more goods as the world's panacea is an ill-advised myth when faced with the scarcity of raw materials. The wisest way to meet the needs of a global society is through an equitable distribution of the world's goods. "Already under way are radical shifts from production to distribution, from supply to demand and from independence to interdependence among nations." (Cornish Rogers, "Global Justice: A Moral Challenge to Religion," *The Christian Century,* June 26, 1974.) It has been apparent now that future competition for resources will be made within a common framework. The impact that we belong to *one world* has become a part of our working consciousness.

It is true that we will always live in tension between the pull of the past and the pressures of the present. Our decisions before conflicting values will always face this inescapable tension. The temptation is to be either optimistic and unrealistic or pessimistic and hopeless in regard to our values, beliefs, and attitudes. In the long run, we need to go beyond simple trade-offs and either/or choices as we create *a new synthesis of values* appropriate for tomorrow's world. We will probably never command a definitive list of values. This places us in the position to constantly reform and reorder our values according to the needs of the time. The search has only begun as we strive consciously toward a realistic community of values in America. The very search itself might well prove to be our salvation from the present value crisis.

The Sign of the Steeple

The search for a community of values will have its greatest impact when integrally related to our institutions. The religious institution, in particular, should assume a leadership role in this area. For too long now the church has taken a back-seat, acting as a reactor to the trends of society rather than as an initiator. Even when the church has appeared to be too socially activistic, it has been in reality a reactor to events and trends triggered by other forces within the society.

Today's need for a community of values provides the church with a vital responsibility. The religious roots underlying a viable set of values should make it clear to all that we can no longer afford to think in parochial terms regarding our religious beliefs.

> We must begin our search for a new value system at that point in our own Western history before our religion was perverted by the worship of acquisitiveness, competition and performance. This means retracing our steps and extricating what we can of the Christianity that informed Western culture

> before the rise of mercantilism, capitalism or industrialization. (Harvey Cox, *The Seduction of the Spirit: The Use and Misuse of People's Religion,* p. 86, Simon & Schuster, New York, 1973.)

We must go beyond thinking in terms of dichotomies, such as spiritual affairs vs. social activism. The time has come to be *wholistic* in our approach—to view salvation as total health, a restoration of the individual along with his environment.

Some have called this concern a reaching out for a "new Eden." Whatever metaphor is used, salvation points us toward a restoration of the totality of life, a reconciliation of the Creator with all of his creation. The Eastern Christians refer to this as *apocatastasis*—a restoration of all life under God. My own personal salvation can have meaning only within this larger context. The importance of this Biblical insight receives added impetus within our global village where my interests and my neighbor's converge.

When the *Journal* writes in its editorial that there is "Dwindling Religious Activism" (January 29, 1973), it is still thinking in either/or terms. "What most people seek in religion," says the *Journal,* " . . . is a broad spiritual direction that will satisfy their metaphysical hunger." Religious activism denies this, according to the *Journal,* since "activism is inadequate to fill that spiritual void which religion alone seems able to satisfy in individual man." The *Journal*'s dichotomized outlook fails to see the wholistic needs of man which an adequate religious response must supply.

Irving Kristol also echoes this concern, when he observes "that it is becoming clearer every day that even those who thought they were content with a religion that was a private affair are themselves discovering that such a religion is existentially unsatisfactory." ("Capitalism, socialism, and nihilism," *Public Interest,* Spring, 1973, p. 12.) Religion that is not wholistic will never satisfy either our metaphysical or physical hunger.

This theme of wholeness will become even more important for religion in the future. According to *U.S. News & World Report* (January 14, 1974), authorities of American religious life in 1994 "foresee churches of the future placing more weight on linking worship directly with solving society's problems, rejecting a cloistered or nonpartisan attitude toward realities of life." Religion is concerned not only with the transcendent dimensions of life, but also with the caprices and contingencies of the physical order.

Ultimately, a wholistic religion places its faith in the meaningfulness of existence, grounded in a God who is able to overcome the chaos created by human sin. *In a Watergate world, the final security of the human spirit rests with God.* "In false religion this ultimate security is prematurely appropriated and corrupted," observes Reinhold Niebuhr (*Beyond Tragedy,* p. 95, Charles Scribner's Sons, 1937), "so that it assures man peace in his sins and not through the forgiveness of his sins." To understand the import of Niebuhr's statement, we need only reflect upon the human situation reported in the pages of the *Journal* and recall the discussion of our previous chapters.

To find ultimate security in the living God is often too gigantic a step for pragmatic individuals who prefer to divide their world into Sundays and Mondays, building up securities in each account. The tragedy is that such persons fail to see that the tapestry of life, while intricately woven and complex, is all-of-one piece, whose final design must be anticipated in faith.

To make us aware of this totality of life, with its imperfections and beauty, is the task of the church. Is the church fulfilling its role? Is it an adequate interpreter of our lives, hopes, values, and frustrations? Is it shedding new insight into our search for a community of values? Is the steeple a sign of hope in our communities? Or is the steeple increasingly up-for-sale in your community? Barry Newman of the *Journal* expressed such a trend in his story, **"For Sale: Brk 3-Story W/9 Rms and 3 Baths; And a Real Nice Steeple"** (December 28, 1970). A growing number of churches in both rural and urban situations will be faced with this problem, unless a clearer understanding of the church's purpose and mission is set forth in each community.

For instance, take the Walnut Avenue Church. Walnut Avenue Church is a case-study example which my students discuss in an attempt to understand the role of the church in today's society. This church has on its rolls some 900 members and is located in a suburban community. Life within the church appears tranquil until lightning strikes and damages the steeple of the church beyond repair.

Replacement of the steeple will cost approximately $50,000. The congregation gradually becomes divided between steeple and non-steeple supporters. "What is a church without a steeple?" argues one side. The other group wishes to raise the $50,000, but prefers to use the money for various innovative mission enterprises in the community at large. A church without a steeple, they insist, can be a church creatively engaged in mission. Exactly what that mission ought to be further complicates the matter.

While Walnut Avenue Church continues to debate the situation, the majority of the membership and citizenry of the community show only passing interest. Church disputes have become "old hat" in an increasingly complex world that is finding the church and its "steeples" irrelevant. Mainline denominations are losing members and have turned unsuccessfully to such projects as "Key 73," a cooperative evangelical drive of Catholics and Protestants to recruit new parishioners as well as to revitalize the old membership already on the rolls.

A psychiatrist once described the church as a hypochondriac widow living behind closed blinds with memories of her dead husband. A hypochondriac, by dictionary definition, is one who exhibits "morbid anxiety over one's own health." Is this what the church has been doing? National denominational assemblies and meetings spend, it seems, an unusual amount of time on introspective questions as they juggle the administrative budgets within their respective departments and pursue new programs of restructuring to cope with the increasing financial crunch. At this rate, will the hypochondriac widow survive?

It is, of course, easy to find fault with the church. Yet, the underlying question here is whether the church is worth saving. Are churches making a significant contribution to society to merit wide public support? Can you envision future model communities designed without churches or synagogues? This might well be the case if the current disinterest in the institutionalism of religion continues and the nostalgic desire for steeples on the horizon diminishes as well.

While the psychiatrist's description of the church is uncomplimentary, it does force us to take fresh notice of what today's church should be. In the first place, the church is not a hypochondriac but an institutional organism that lives in the world. Her aim is to spend herself in mission; she has often been described as a servant-people. Second, the church is not a widow but a joyful and expectant bride waiting the arrival of her groom. Third, the church should never rest behind closed blinds, but as God's people she should be moving out to proclaim, describe, and demonstrate the shalom, or peace of God, to men and women in the world. Her message is one of light and life, not of night and death. Fourth, the church should not be preoccupied with memories of her "dead husband" but should worship a living Presence. The master of the household of faith is the living Lord.

The local church is the basic institutional unit upon which hospitals, schools, colleges, seminaries, social centers, and the like are dependent. The decline in influence of the local church is a threatening experience for all these related institutions. There is no escape, it seems, from the institutionalism of religion in some form or another. Even the Jesus Movement and Catholic Pentecostalism are learning that there is no place to go without an institutional framework. As Martin Marty of the University of Chicago has pointed out, "nothing institutionalized itself more rapidly than did anti-institutional protest movements" (*A.D.,* November, 1972). In time, every man's faith points to some idea of a "church" where two or more individuals share some beliefs in common. In short, the question isn't whether the local church is worth saving, but in what form will it continue to exist.

Each aspect of the psychiatrist's description of the church is exactly opposite to what the church should be according to the Biblical standards. It is almost as if the church has projected a reverse image of herself, as if one were looking at a photographic negative rather than a positive print. Most of us know what the church ought to be, but we either cast it off as an ideal or impractical model for our day, or else we lose track of its purpose among our pressing daily affairs. This collective amnesia within the church and within society is currently one of our gravest problems.

To regain our identity as believers is the mission of the church today. Recently a neighbor offered me a ride from the airport along with two of his colleagues. When I was introduced as a Presbyterian minister teaching in a seminary, it was revealed that all the men in the car, each unbeknown to the others, were also Presbyterians. Although it was a pleasant experience, this brought home to me the duality of the *private and public life* which laymen maintain and clergymen often nurture. This way of life today is accepted without serious question as a necessary means for survival in "the secular city."

What hope is there in the dilemma of duality confronted by clergy and laity? Hope lies, it seems to me, at the level of personal encounter. Mission is not simply a programmed and systematic enterprise carried on by the institutional church. Neither the "First City Church" nor "St. Joseph's on the Hillside" as institutions can become instruments of mission without persons. Mission begins whenever and wherever individuals take it upon themselves to raise questions of life and death with their neighbors in the context of genuine concern. Each time this takes place, we are overcoming the gap which currently exists between private and public life. We are then taking the proper wholistic outlook.

The primary task of the church is to encourage individuals in substantive dialogue, while providing nurture through worship, study, and fellowship for the sake of mission. The church is under obligation to throw light upon the numerous challenges of the day. To meet these challenges with freshness rather than fear makes it necessary for us not only to be informed but to learn how to express our convictions as well. The call is out for each of us to be practicing grass roots theologians—professing believers who find ourselves *relating* formally or informally, in our professions or avocations, in word or deed, the Word of God to the human situation.

Once believers see themselves engaged in mission, the church is well on the road to recovery. For the recovery to be sustained, it is incumbent upon local pastors to share more completely their administrative responsibilities with the laity, who in many cases are better qualified. The corporation executive has become the model for the ministry in far too many instances. Organizational administration is important, but is that the primary task of an ordained minister? Theological education is an expensive detour if administration is one's goal. Unfortunately, many ministers would be lost in the parish without the task of administration. No matter how often these ministers complain publicly about administrative chores, they would not want to relinquish them.

In fact, the "happy pastor" often appears to be involved in some building program where administration and its related activities consume almost his entire time. During the building process, the minister is able to bury his lingering guilt feelings toward his theological responsibilities. Some pastors even consider involvement with theology too risky an affair, especially during a building or restructuring program. Theology divides, doesn't it? Thus theology is quickly dismissed as being divisive, a non-contributive factor to the "life, unity, and purity" of the congregation. The heresy of the contemporary church and her ministry lies in an excessive preoccupation with business and public relations without theological direction.

Who is it in our society that makes significant and prophetic statements about the epic events of our times? Often it is astronauts, artists, novelists, newscasters, politicians, but for the most part certainly not ministers. Ministers have undermined their vital role as opinion makers in society. Harried, tired, and ill-prepared, they have become an inarticulate voice in a world seeking purpose and hope. Where are the pastor-theologians, the interpreters of the Word of God within the events of human life?

Without such theologizing, the church will wed herself to the culture of the day and be a widow within each succeeding age, always trying to catch up but seldom providing leadership. Actually, the dilemma of the Walnut Avenue Church is really an opportunity for theological growth for pastor and parishioners. Hopefully, their struggle will result in a healthier, more vital church that knows why it exists. It will then be in a better position to provide leadership in our search for abiding values.

Second Thoughts on the Good Life

In one way or another, we have been asking throughout our discussion the question, "What is the good life?" According to Professor Richard Herrnstein of Harvard University in a syndicated newspaper series on "America and the Future of Man," the good life is based upon a measure of material success, and the esteem of one's peers.

Life, Herrnstein observes, is a mix between rewards and frustrations with much competitive struggle and inequalities in the process. The result is a society of winners and losers. In the same series of articles Carl Rogers invites us to transcend these realities, to create a parallel process of openness with ourselves and with others, and ultimately to establish guidelines which will free us from depersonalized institutional authorities in our search for self-fulfillment. For Rogers, the good life is based upon a realistic appraisal and acceptance of one's self.

To a large extent I find myself agreeing with both Herrnstein and Rogers. However, in the long run, both of their views of "the good life" may tend to be too elitist and too private, a tendency which the *Journal* also shares. There must be caution in positioning an individual as the primary determiner of what is "good" and "bad" for himself. While the pitfalls of institutional authorities exist in a Watergate world, the fact remains that private and public dimensions of authority must co-exist together. Every community, including those which exalt the individual as the highest authority, will have the need to organize. The institutional life-style of an organized community holds in large measure the key to the good life.

Most organized communities, however, are nothing more than the rationalization of power. If power is the end goal, then the enhancement of life is only a means, and we will become more deeply immersed in the morass of a world such as the Watergate world. An organized community that fails to bring the good life closer to its people is failing in its ultimate mission. It is only introducing more suffering to the human scene. While there is no escape from suffering, Brazilian theologian Rubem Alves (*Tomorrow's Child,* p. 203, Harper & Row, 1972) notes that "suffering without hope produces resentment and despair. Hope without suffering creates illusions, naïveté, and drunkenness." If we are then to go beyond the *Journal*'s gospel of struggling individualism based upon a common sense realism, organized communities will need to have their aims clearly in mind—namely, *a minimization of suffering and the maximization of a higher quality of life.*

The clue to the maximization of a higher quality of life lies with the organized community that exemplifies openness and trust—values which have been sorely bankrupt in our society of late. To achieve openness and trust, an organized community will need as its base an underlying foundation of practicing forgiveness. *Forgiveness is the human way of loving and giving support to each other.* We can't say we accept each other unless we have the compassion to reach out concretely, forgiving the human faces and events which surround us. Can anyone go through a week of living without forgiving and being forgiven? The absence of this forgiving spirit rather than economics is our greatest barrier in reaching the good life.

Some companies are actively trying to promote this atmosphere of acceptance through the employment of clergymen in their organizations. Bill Paul of the *Journal* describes this in his story, "*Matters of Faith:* **At Some Companies, Every Day Is Marked by Religious Exercises**—Key Decisions Are Preceded by Prayer; Workers Hear Sermons, Attend Services, A Chaplain on the Payroll." (April 5, 1973.) Other organizations are expressing similar concerns through the aid of psychologists and psychiatrists.

A revitalized religious institution can be one of the most important organizations in leading a community to enhance its quality of life beyond material measurements. But how many are models where openness, trust, and forgiveness are practiced?

Most of us work hard to conceal our hurts as we come to church in our Sunday best, designed to hide rather than to reveal ourselves. Each of us wishes to appear to his neighbor as a "successful" Christian. The truth may well be that we are in a state of hell. Hell is the experience of standing out in the cold carrying our burdens alone. The invitation to come in from the cold is what the new life in Christ is all about. This is the church's message.

Is this Gospel according to Christ too good to be true? Is there really a future with Christ? Does the cross make sense in a Watergate world? These are the questions that haunt Christians and non-Christians alike. We are deciding for or against the way of the cross each day of our lives. Are we so bound to static structures, bent on maintaining power and the status quo, that their reality supersedes the reality of Christ? In John le Carré's novel, *The Spy Who Came in from the Cold,* we capture a glimpse of our existence. The story is about a brilliant spy, Leamas, whose mission revealed the strikingly contemporary tension of our existence. It is the tension of a committed man unable to come to terms with the utterly ruthless machine he serves. Leamas facetiously asks, "What do you think spies are: priests, saints and martyrs?" (p. 246) Substitute "Christians" for "spies," and we could raise the same question. "What do you think Christians are: priests, saints and martyrs?" "God, forbid!" we reply. As a result, we have promoted a split-level church as Christians—a church of the committed and the half-committed.

Rabbi Abraham Joshua Heschel, whom Edmund Fuller of the *Journal* rightly describes as "a man for all seasons because his vision was rooted in his worship of a God for all seasons" ("Rabbi Heschel's Heritage of Wonder and Awe," February 2, 1973), pinpoints man's most serious problem—the issue of martyrdom. "Is there anything worth dying for? We can only live the truth if we have the power to die for it. Suicide is an escape from evil and surrender to absurdity. A martyr is a witness to the holy in spite of evil absurdity." How many of us have chosen to view our commitments from this perspective? Most of us seek, it seems, a Christianity without a cross. The possibility of sharing *the cross* is an integral part of our baptismal vows. There is no escape from suffering; there is a cross in every household. We are indeed the fellowship of the broken–hearted. The church ought to be the center where our wounded, scarred, and unhealed feelings can be expressed in openness and in love.

Within our households we are constantly being pulled between the secular and sacred styles of life. Are these two styles of life really one? There is much confusion about this in the civil religion of the day. Most of us claim to be committed to a "heavenly vision" while tied to an "earthly existence." The Eastern Christian tradition has long testified, through centuries of hardship, that the church is an island of heaven upon the earth. In life, the believer will always struggle between these two realms, heaven and earth. To deny the tension is to be unrealistic; to reduce the tension is to be so "heavenly minded" that we are of no earthly use. The truth is that we are immersed in layers of the secular and sacred at every given moment—from discussing our annual church budget to the Watergate affair, from the issue of amnesty to the numerous domestic squabbles that we encounter each day.

Interpreting a Christian style of life is more difficult than many of us are willing to admit. In our increasing awareness of this, seminaries today are developing classes which employ a case study approach. Taking authentic human experiences and dilemmas, like the Walnut Avenue Church, students learn to identify the theological issues at stake as they seek a Christian response for that particular situation. Not to admit the complexities of life is to live in a dream world of non-tension that is neither secular nor sacred. In which direction have you resolved the secular-sacred tension? The challenge is out to "swing with our age" and its numerous counter-cultures. The pressure is on, and no one is out of its circle of gravity.

It appears at times that unless we are swinging couples, we are not with it. Unless we decorate our coffee tables with a copy of *Playboy* or *Penthouse,* we are only admitting our inhibitions. Unless our children show early popularity with the opposite sex, we worry about their attractiveness. Unless we express our passions, we are accused of not having any feelings. Unless we own a slick automobile, we lack ambition and drive. Which of us is not tempted to see life in terms of these secular realities alone? Which of us, including the *Journal,* is not tempted to arrange our priorities according to the "common sense" ways of our day? Not to go along with the currents of the day leaves us out in the cold. It makes us feel like "squares," a feeling which is a middle-class hell of its own.

Plagued by our doubts, questions, and confusion, we wonder whether there really is a God. Our faith at times cools off as we take quick dips into the mainstream of our culture. Of course, we still want to do what is right. God knows we are decent people! Our tempers fly at times, but isn't that human? We continue to nurture a competitive rather than a cooperative spirit in our children, because we feel it is right. On occasions, our malicious thoughts toward others surprise and even scare us.

We find ourselves remarkably empathetic to the philosophy of quick revenge as expressed in Mario Puzo's book, *Godfather.* It's a more direct approach in dealing with one's enemy than the long-suffering advocated by the Apostle Paul, which leaves us exhausted and frustrated. Behind all our feelings is the threatening notion that God doesn't exist. As a consequence, the invitation to accept the Gospel according to Christ for one's life-style sounds at the moment hollow and distant, as the frosty winds push us further out into the cold.

God lives, but the feeling lingers within us that this God has isolated himself from the everyday concerns of human existence. God is absent as eighteenth century deism once proclaimed. Having created us, he has now abandoned us to our ways. He has left us wandering as lost pilgrims suffering out in the cold. Out of despondency and doubt we have been warming ourselves at other fireplaces sponsored by false gods, but the chill in our bones is still there. We are still restless and cold. We need special outfitting to effectively battle the *cold war* which exists in our lives. This clothing, Biblically described, consists of compassion, kindness, lowliness, meekness, patience, long-suffering, forgiveness, love, and thankfulness. The total design of the outfit describes the well-dressed believer.

How would we describe the outfit we are wearing today? Where is our compassion today? If compassion is termed as concern for others, how extensive is our circle of concern? What limits have been placed on our compassion quantitatively and qualitatively? Our compassion often doesn't stretch even within our families, let alone beyond them. The most we do for others amounts to a first-aid approach, including our foreign aid to others.

As for kindness, lowliness, and meekness, we know that we aren't in first place. But, like the Avis ads, "we try harder" than our neighbors, don't we? At least with that effort we hope to find some favor with God. God knows we try to be patient and long-suffering with our neighbors, but to ask us to practice forgiveness toward our enemies may be going a bit too far. There are limits to "playing Christian," aren't there? We have concluded long ago in our saner moments that heaven must consist of unforgiving, unreconciled persons; otherwise, we wouldn't make it. Hell for many persons is other people. The film *Happy Birthday, Wanda June* based on Kurt Vonnegut's play reveals the inhabitants of heaven as a mixed crowd. Everyone is there—from Hitler's henchmen to Martin Luther King, Jr., to ten-year-old Wanda June. Heaven appears as an extension of our earthly hell. If this is the case, then apparently we are held together by our hate rather than by our love. "Those who hate together stay together" certainly seems to be the unfortunate theme of our lives.

Forgiveness and love, undoubtedly, sounds like pious language until we experience it. "Forgive and forget" is an empty cliché. It never works in practice, nor is it necessarily Biblical. *The Biblical emphasis is upon forgiveness, not forgetting.* Forgiveness involves pain. To forgive without forgetting is painful. There is always a cross at every forgiving encounter. To forgive without experiencing the pain of healing is not really to forgive. *Forgiveness is the human way of loving each other.* Love in abstraction is an affront to God and man.

Finally, looking beyond the gospel according to *The Wall Street Journal,* the good life depends on a spirit of forgiveness in the context of celebration and thankfulness. The test of radical faith is seen in direct ratio to our capacity to forgive and to give thanks in everything. Only by these means can we experience the peace of God to rule our restlessness.

The gospel of Christ points beyond immediate survival through "avoid illusions, be realistic." Through Christ, we acknowledge our shortcomings and affirm the Creator's endowment in everyone. *The Wall Street Journal* contributes much to our understanding of human existence; however, it is the gospel of Christ which enables us to fulfill our humanity.